Christine Burns

Van Life: From Da

How to Quit your 9-!
Down by the River

By: Alexandra Van Steen with input from Frankie McCullough aka FnAVanLife

This book is dedicated to everyone who helped make our van life dreams come true. Whether you worked on our builds directly, helped support us emotionally, or followed our journey online, we couldn't have done it without you. From the bottom of our hearts, thank you.

As a thank you to the beautiful planet that makes van life possible and oh so enjoyable, 10% of the earnings from this book will be donated to environmental causes.

Introduction

So you want to live van life? The open road is calling your name. You're ready to break out of your cubicle, the birdcage of your 9 to 5 existence and spread your wings. The idea of traveling like a turtle with all the comforts of home on your back is incredibly appealing. You get to visit the most glorious locations your wheels can take you and never have to set up a tent or worry about rain. You can explore mountains and forests, waterfalls and hot springs, beaches and bohemian towns. Whatever your tastes, you can find a location that will make all your wanderlust dreams come true. You just have to get into your tiny home on wheels and drive there.

I caught the van life bug bad. I spent the first 30 years of my life doing what I was supposed to. I went to school, graduated on the honor roll and got right to work. I never had that travel bug people talked about. While friends were heading off for a year or more in Australia, Europe or Asia, I did the safe thing.

Got a job in an office and put all my energies into "getting ahead" and saving for the future. I didn't see the point of traveling for extended periods when I could be making a steady paycheck, socking away money in my retirement accounts, taking one-week holidays from time to time and making my parents proud.

I excelled at administrative support and carved out a nice living working for a top executive in New York City. Over 10 years I had climbed to the top of my career path from Receptionist to Executive Assistant. I should have been happy. I should have been looking for the next corporate mountain to climb. But all I felt was hollow.

Was *this* it? Was I really going to continue giving 40 hours a week to someone else? I looked around and saw unhappy faces, stress lines, people dreaming of their next vacation and counting down to retirement. I was tired of planning a vacation as soon as I got home from one. I was tired of figuring out how many vacation days I had for the year and realizing how few were left.

That's when I discovered van life. On our first date, Frankie mentioned that he was going to be leaving New York in a few months to travel by car across the country. My immediate reaction was "I want to do that with you" which I stashed away in my mind not wanting to sound insane as we had just met an hour before. What came out of my mouth was something like "wow that sounds awesome" but this new idea had come into my existence with excitement and wonder.

As soon as this bug was my planted in my head, I did a deep dive into the internet world of what it would be like to drive across the country. I was immediately immersed into the van life movement. The gorgeous builds. The amazing RVs that looked like million-dollar mansions. The mountains in the background. The beaches from beyond the backdoors. The freedom. The possibility.

I was completely hooked. As I do with most things I want in my life, I started a spreadsheet. What would be the costs? Where would we go? How many miles per gallon were we going to get? I watched video after video, imagining myself as the intrepid adventurer. Could I really give up my life in New York City to travel the open road? Could I quit my job and leave the comforts of home for the complete unknown? The answer was a resounding *yes*.

As my relationship with Frankie developed, he conveniently decided to postpone his road trip for another year. That would give us more time to see if our relationship could handle life in a tiny box (first our NYC apartment and then the van) and also to save money for and build our tiny home on wheels.

When I presented Frankie with my detailed spreadsheet chronicling the estimated costs for a year on the road and, detailing how much we would need to save to afford it, his solo adventure happily became a duo trip.

As we dove head first into shopping for our vehicle, building our tiny home on wheels and then hitting the open road, I realized there was a ton of information out there, but nothing compiled into an easy all-encompassing guide that would take us from daydream to dream life.

That's what I'm going to create for you here. This book will outline the steps you'll need to take to buy, build and live in your tiny home on wheels. With tips ranging from how to choose the right toilet to where to sleep on the road, I've got you covered. If you're a dreamer and a planner like I am, this guide will help you tremendously. And with tons of technical input from Frankie, who does most of the tricky work on the road, we've got you covered.

My dream for you is as big as my dream was for myself. I want you to love your life and live freely. Frankie and I believe van life is the perfect way to experience the world and we hope you'll step outside the norm to join us on the road.

We'd love to meet you in person or hear from you online. Feel free to find us on Instagram @FnAVanlife or contact me on my website www.fnavanlife.com.

"Be fearless in the pursuit of what sets your soul on fire." — Jennifer Lee

Why Van Life?

As more people choose this lifestyle all over the world, one has to wonder, why is van life so appealing to so many? Of course, everyone has their own highly personal reasons but from the many people I've met living this lifestyle, there are a few commonalities.

The first is reason is freedom. Most vanlifers have worked traditional jobs and been part of the traditional system. Perhaps they owned their own home, worked a corporate job and were generally living the way society expects. Get good grades, graduate from school, get a good job, get married, have kids, work hard all your life, retire, *then* you can travel.

At some point, the crushing reality that your hopes and dreams don't matter, that corporate profits are more important, and that two weeks of vacation per year just doesn't cut it, pushes people to look for alternatives. Van life is a way to break free of the traditional norms of society, forever or just for a while, to be able to see more of the world and satisfy your wanderlust.

Being able to travel for extended periods of time without the hassle of having to check into hostels or live out of a suitcase is spectacular. You get to experience ever-changing scenery and yet fall asleep in the same bed every night. You have all the comforts of home but at the same time all the adventure of travel. In my opinion it's the best of both worlds. In a COVID world, many seasoned travelers have turned to van life as a way to continue the adventure within their own country.

I've seen countless "influencers" join van life in the last few months because it's currently the safest, if not only way to travel. As someone considering this lifestyle (you wouldn't be reading this book if you weren't!) you can rest assured you'll be in good company on the road.

Next up, vanlifers generally don't want to carry the debt burden of traditional life. If your expenses are low, you don't need to make that much money. Life becomes simple on the road as you only have to worry about basic necessities. You no longer have a huge rent or mortgage payment, multiple cars to pay off and insure, daily commuter costs or even just the subscriptions that pile up.

Many vanlifers choose to live this way because it allows them to save more money. As some of us still work full time jobs or earn money as entrepreneurs, imagine how much extra money you would have each month if you didn't have to pay for your housing. This frees up so much capital and allows you to invest in things that are more important to you, like perhaps experiences.

Of course, the sexiest reason to choose van life is the adventure it holds.

Imagine waking up in a new and stunning location everyday (well most days, some days you wake up at Walmart). The excitement of planning a new route, of conquering another mountain or surfing another wave. Most vanlifers love to be in the outdoors whether that's for hiking, biking, fishing, boating, climbing, snowboarding/skiing, kiting, kayaking, portaging, camping, skateboarding or even just simply walking through nature.

A van life van generally has a stash of gear to assist in these adventurous pursuits with boards of all kinds, wetsuits, ropes, helmets, poles and whatever else is needed for favorite activities. Many vanlifers get into this lifestyle so they can take their sport to newer heights or just be able to do it more often in exciting locations.

And even if you're not into sport, the adventure of visiting new places all the time is incredibly intoxicating.

The other side of the coin is that some people don't choose van life, van life is thrust upon them. Their housing situation becomes unstable for whatever reason and they decide to live in their vehicle.

This vanlifer might not have the time or money to build out a rig as gloriously as some, but set up doesn't have to be complicated or costly to qualify as a van life rig. Even in dire situations, this lifestyle offers freedom and adventure.

Freedom from high rent payments so money earned is money saved. Freedom from unhealthy relationships that may have be a catalyst for leaving your housing situation. Adventure in finding new places to sleep every night, finding bathrooms and showers. And of course, the adventure of exploring the outdoors and starting a new life full of possibility. On our podcast we ask vanlifers the simple question, why van life?

Their answers are all as unique as they are but the themes of freedom, adventure and cost savings come up again and again. Whether you're thinking about van life as a one-year escape from the real world, a temporary layover before you find your next home, or your new forever lifestyle, the lessons in this book will guide you to make the most of your journey.

"The life you have led doesn't need to be the only life you have." — Anna Quindlen

Quit Your Job to Live the Dream

This was by far the scariest part of our journey. Frankie and I both worked decent jobs in New York City. Frankie was an HVAC technician and I was an Executive Assistant. We both liked our jobs, our coworkers and bosses and we liked the paychecks.

Each week bled into the next, the countdown to the next long weekend or vacation was endless. But we would come back from that vacation, even more exhausted than when we left. Emails piled up, unanswered voicemail, more stress. Any relaxation we achieved quickly disappeared and the countdown to the next holiday began.

Years could have slipped through our fingers living like this - in fact, they did.

Ten years working the same job with the same company for Frankie and the same type of job with a few different firms for me. When I looked at the people ten years ahead of me, I didn't like what I saw.

Now in addition to counting down to their next vacation day, they were counting down years until retirement so they could actually enjoy their lives. I don't know about you, but I'd much rather enjoy my life now and not wait for an unpromised future.

Choosing the timing to quit our jobs was very specific. We made sure not to tell anyone at the company too early for fear that we would end up on our asses before we could afford to be. We needed the security of our jobs to save as much money as we could to build our van and have a stash of cash to travel with.

We needed time to take all the steps we're about to outline in the next few chapters: to build our van; sell our assets; put in notice for our apartment; and make sure we were ready for what lay ahead.

Think about the timing of any bonuses or payouts you want to take advantage of. For example, for my 401K match I had to be employed on December 31st of the year to get paid out for the full year I had just worked. I could quit January 1st and make that money but not a day before.

Our annual bonuses paid out in April so I was willing to walk away from that lump sum. I figured I was leaving anyways and would have felt guilty taking the money and running.

Frankie didn't really have any payouts to consider. He generally got a Christmas bonus but the few hundred dollars wasn't worth it to him to be able to spend his last few weeks in New York building the van.

Frankie gave just over 2 months' notice. When he told his management team, they were so happy for him to live his adventure and offered him his job back whenever he wanted. Secretly, they were all rolling their eyes.

Why would he give up such a good job to live in a van and essentially be homeless? Little did they know that less than a year later, all their jobs would be on the line because of COVID and living in a van down by the river was looking pretty good.

I also gave just under 2 months' notice that I was leaving my job. I wanted to wait until my 401K was fully vested (something you should consider) so the day of my five-year anniversary with the firm, I put in my notice. I should say, I walked into my boss' office sobbing and unable to make words.

I was so incredibly nervous about quitting my job. My boss was a lovely man and he and I had an excellent working relationship. I was worried he would be upset with me, disappointed, but just like Frankie's team, he was happy for me.

Of course, he was sad to see me go but he agreed that work is just work and you have to live your life the way you see fit.

Both our companies threw us farewell parties and sent us off in style. My boss even arranged for me to still get my bonus in April and put me on sabbatical instead of just quitting so if van life didn't work out, I could always come back. Since then, my boss has quit the company too, realizing that a job is just a job. Family and time are much more valuable.

People think that 9 to 5 jobs are stable, sturdy and dependable. You've got a retirement plan and you will be comfortable all your life if you just give 40 hours or more a week to the company. Of course, we know this isn't true.

Companies can be downsized, amalgamated, sold or relocated. Scandal and fraud bring down even the biggest firms. Retirement plans disappear overnight. And if COVID has taught us anything it's that the status quo can be ripped out from under our feet at a moment's notice.

Leaving the security of your job might be one of the biggest band-aids you'll ever need to rip off in your whole life, but I promise, it is so worth it.

You'll learn from this book how to live with less, be happy with experience over materialism and forge a new path to earning income on your own time. All that plus you get to experience wonders of the world many never will.

Consider how little you actually get to see on a two-week vacation. Two of those days are spent in transit to and from the destination. Even if you have a packed itinerary, which will exhaust you, you haven't even scratched the surface of a place.

You've likely only have visited the tourist locations that guidebooks recommend. You haven't allowed the flow to take you on adventures to new and glorious places.
You can always get another job. You can't get back time wasted building someone else's dreams.

"And then there is the most dangerous risk of all — the risk of spending your life not doing what you want on the bet you can buy yourself the freedom to do it later." — Randy Komisar

The Budget

As sexy as a budget is, this is where all van life dreams begin. If you think you're going to be cruising across the country in a luxury Class A RV complete with white leather couches, stone lined showers and a full marble kitchen, but your bank account struggles to afford an $8 latte, you'd be best to rethink your dreams.

Frankie's pre-budget plan for his vehicle was a brand-new Jeep Gladiator with a brand-new Mini Max Pro trailer towing behind. This would have set him back approximately $50,000 for the Jeep and $20,000 for the teardrop trailer. As he was going to finance the purchases, he would have a large monthly payment to make while on the road.

These payments would significantly cut down on the length of our travels as we did not plan to work. The whole point of van life is to get rid of your rent payment or mortgage. If you trade one monthly payment for another, have you really freed yourself from anything?

On the flip side, if you've worked out how to make money on the road and have a steady income, what's the harm in financing a new/newer vehicle? A newer van should have a lot fewer mechanical issues to worry about and might even still be under warranty. Depending on your mechanical prowess, this might be the better option for you. Again, you need to know and crunch your budget numbers to see if this is feasible.

I read an article the other day that was warning how financially dangerous van life can be. A retiree had purchased a 1999 Thomas school bus and spent $45,000 converting it into her tiny home. She spent the majority of her savings on this project but didn't consider that a 1999 school bus might come with a fair number of mechanical repairs. She spent another lump of cash fixing the bus engine and at the end of the year found herself $10,000 in debt. Don't be that lady!

After I put Frankie's dream rig figures into a budget and outlined that he would have to save almost $6,000 per month for a full year to cover the extravagant costs, he quickly changed his mind. We decided on a much more reasonable $6,000 total for the vehicle and $5,000 for the build (these were not our final numbers - I'll tell you those shortly).

I plopped these numbers into a budget that estimated all the other costs I assumed we would incur over the course of our travels. After watching tons of videos that broke down the cost of living on the road, I felt I had good information to base my budget on.

I have a complete breakdown of these expenses and our actual budget for download on our website (https://fnavanlife.com/budget-to-quit-your-job-for-extended-travel/), but in a nutshell, they included:

- Vehicle purchase
- Registration
- Build expenses
- Health insurance
- Car insurance
- Groceries/ Restaurants
- Gas
- Phones
- Internet
- Coffee shops
- Engine maintenance
- Gym membership
- Hotel nights
- Camp sites
- Excursions/activities
- Personal care products
- Annual park/snowboard passes

Other items you might need to consider that didn't apply to us could include:

- Monthly vehicle cost
- Child care costs
- Pet care costs
- Camp ground memberships
- Streaming services (Netflix, etc.)
- Cell phone booster
- Mobile internet
- Alcohol

The general rule with setting up a budget is to overestimate the expenses you think you will have. It's better to save too much than to save too little. The good news is that life on the road can be quite reasonable. Of course, you can find ways to live luxuriously in any city in the world. Eating out, paying for once in a lifetime experiences, staying in expensive camp sites and the like will dwindle any budget more quickly.

On the other hand, cooking your own meals, finding free experiences and stealth camping cost next to nothing. You know yourself best, so when putting your budget together, decide where you are willing to be conservative and where you need to splurge for your own sanity and wellbeing (and some awesome adventures).

If you're not sure how much to put down for a certain budget item, look back at your spending for the prior 3 months. Do you generally spend $300 a month on groceries or $600? $500 a month eating out and at bars? Assume you'll continue to spend about the same or a little bit more when it comes to food. For other items like health care, you might have to do some research.

Personally, I've always had health insurance through my work and never needed to get a plan on the open market. This was eye opening for me and I wouldn't have been able to set a budget amount without doing some research. Even if you live in a country with free health care, you might need to budget for traveler's insurance. When you cross a boarder, your governments plan likely won't cover you anymore.

If you have an idea of where you want to travel, you can also pull costs for bucket list or local must do activities from the internet. If you know you must have a helicopter tour of the Grand Canyon, you can easily gather prices and budget for this type of experience. For us, we knew we wanted to snowboard so we factored the cost of the annual snowboarding passes into the budget.

Once you've got a total estimated cost of monthly expenses, multiply that amount by the number of months you want to travel. This gives you the final figure of how much you need to save to be able to travel without earning any additional income as you go.

Of course, if you're going to work on the road (we'll discuss nomadic earning later in this book) you don't need to save quite as much up front, but it's always good to have a nest egg. You never know when the next flat tire or leaky radiator is going to set you back a few dinero.

A general budget guideline is to have 3 to 6 months' worth of expenses in your bank account at all times. This will float you if you can't find/don't want to work or have an unexpected expense (think mandatory engine repair). When your bank account is starting to get that low, you'll need to start to think about heading home or ways to earn cash on the road.

Perhaps I'm a bit too fiscally responsible. I log every dollar we spend and sit Frankie down to budget meetings all the time. If you're someone who is more fancy-free, this advice might seem extreme. Hopefully we can meet in the middle.

You don't have to have all your money saved - heck you don't have to have any money saved. Many people fall into van life because of unfortunate circumstances. I've seen plenty of posts online about people who are going to be evicted at the end of the month and need a van now. These vanlifers are the ultimate budgeters because they only have X amount of dollars and that's it. I hope this will never be you but if it is, rest assured you're entering a very thrifty lifestyle.

Your van life experience will be much more satisfying, adventurous and longer if you put some preplanning into your bank account even if this means staying at a job you don't love just a little bit longer to save as much as you can. Frankie and I both worked and saved for a full year before we actually hit the road.

It was painful at times. I would often lament about how I just wanted to be on the road already, how exhausted I was working full time and building the van. But it was all worth it because now we're super comfortable, have no financial worries and can truly enjoy van life.

"All journeys have secret destinations of which the traveler is unaware." — Martin Buber

Your Rig

This is the first and potentially biggest question of your van life adventure, what are you going to call home? The options are endless as any vehicle can technically qualify - van life rigs come in all shapes and sizes. Vanlifers live in everything from tiny cars, SUVs, minivans, flatbed trucks with houses built on the back, to teardrop trailers, high-top vans, school buses, ambulances, RVs, box trucks and more.

Move into anything with at least 4 wheels and an engine and you're welcomed into the van life family. There are some purists that think only a Sprinter or similar high-top van count, but I'm much more open minded about the whole thing. We all want similar things from life and all face similar challenges when it comes to living on the road, so, who cares what you drive? The more rigs on the road the merrier.

For our first van life rig, we went with a 2003 Dodge Sprinter with a high-top roof. One of our biggest desires was to be able to stand fully upright. I didn't want to be crouching down all the time or making dinner on my knees.

We've seen a lot of builds in these shorter vehicles and the people really don't seem to mind. You get used to your space very quickly, no matter how big or small, even if you can't stand upright. But for us, it was a deal breaker as this was going to be our full-time home.

The reason we got an older vehicle was because of our budget. We only had $6,000 to spend on our van so had to look at older models. We searched on Craigs List, eBay, Auto Trader and Facebook Market Place. We visited a few from Craigs List but found eBay too scary (I'm going to bid on something on the other side of the country without ever having seen it in person?).

I have since met people who have been just fine with eBay so don't let me sway you. Auto Trader was too expensive as it's mainly dealer or newer vans. Facebook Market Place had the widest selection of used vehicles at reasonable prices.

We could also easily expand our search to wider geographic areas that we could still drive to and it was reassuring to be able to speak directly to the seller.

Before we bought our van, we went to see about 15 other rigs. At first, we thought we wanted an RV because we wouldn't have to build the inside since it was already done.

I imagined those beautiful rigs I saw on Pinterest and Instagram - all white interiors with big kitchens and colorful throw blankets.

The reality, in our price range anyways, were very brown, dark wooded, moldy carpeted shit holes with rotting roofs. We toyed with the idea of gutting the whole thing and rebuilding it the way we wanted, but then what was the point of getting an RV? We may as well just start with a blank canvas.

Next, we looked at ambulances because these builds looked so cool online. Plus, we saw ads for really cheap used ambulances. May as well check them out! Sadly, in a lot full of 200+ ambulances, there were only 4 in our price range (the stated price on the ad I might add). One didn't run and the other 3 were all too short to stand in. They did have more expensive models that would have fit our requirements, but after learning these rigs get roughly 7 miles to the gallon because of their weight, we left empty handed.

This led us into the world of Sprinters, ProMasters and Transits. These are by far the most popular options for building out your own van. Depending on where you're searching for your vehicle, the price of these rigs will vary greatly.

Some of our broad searches would return vehicles that looked perfect and were priced fairly. We would get all excited until we realized that getting that particular vehicle would involve a flight to Kansas. New York City area prices were incredibly inflated (much like the price of everything in NYC).

We had to expand our search to include vehicles that would be a 4+ hour drive away just to get a reasonable price.

The search to find the vehicle of your dreams is honestly an emotional roller coaster. We'd search all week long to set up viewings for the weekend because of our work schedule.

We'd follow up and text to make sure we weren't driving hours in vain. We'd find out on route or the night before that the vehicle had already sold. Sellers would ghost us. Vans we thought were going to be amazing turned out to be crap. We had our hopes dashed time and again.

I found this so frustrating. I would go into the day thinking "we're going to find our van today!" then come home empty handed. Were we ever going to find the right rig for us?

Over the months it took to find Lolo our 2003 Dodge Sprinter, we developed some tips to keep in mind when shopping for a used vehicle:

- You must be proactive, don't wait for sellers to get back to you, stay on top of them
- Look the vehicle over thoroughly even if you don't know anything about vehicles you can easily spot rust, body damage, etc.
- Ask for service records of oil changes and general maintenance
- Get a CarFax report to see if it was in any accidents
- Look up the VIN to make sure nothing crazy has happened to that van
- Look under the engine to see if there are spots of oil on the road or visible leaks
- Drive the car for at least 10 miles listening closely for anything that seems off and watching for check engine lights, if they were reset, they will pop after 10 miles
- Start the car cold (not been running and already hot) to make sure it turns over easily
- Check for rust all over but especially under the vehicle. Surface rust is okay and will scratch off easily, deep rust will fracture/fall apart (avoid that – tap a screw driver to the bottom of the truck to test this).
- Check for water leaks in the body. Old RVs have a tendency to have leaky roofs and even box trucks can have leaky seams.
- Make sure the owner has a "clean title" which means there are no outstanding debts on the car and it's fully owned by them

- Look at the exhaust fumes - in diesel some black smoke at start up is normal but you generally want the fumes to be clear not smoky (this can indicate bigger issues)
- Check the oil (red oil dipsticks should be checked when the engine is hot and yellow dipsticks when the engine is cold)
- Always look under the hood for signs of splattered oil or obviously rotten hoses
- To really be sure of what you're getting, you can ask for the vehicle to be taken to get looked over by a mechanic or bring a mechanic or car savvy friend with you to the potential purchase
- Is the current owner able to provide any government required safety certifications (where applicable)

If you know nothing about car engines, like me, buying a used vehicle can be intimidating. You don't want to spend your money and end up with a lemon! With the tips above you should be in a pretty good place and you can always Google things like "how to check oil".

If you have a friend or partner who's more knowledgeable, have them check the engine over. If you are a member of a gym, church or community group, ask around for a trustworthy mechanic that would be willing to look the vehicle over for free.

Having to make a few simple upgrades is not an issue. Buying a vehicle whose engine is going to die any mile now is not good.

Also note, diesel engines are a lot more complicated and specialized that regular engines. There are many car mechanics who won't work on diesel engines so you have to locate a specialist who knows them well.

You can learn a lot online from looking up the make and model of your vehicle and common issues they have. That way you'll know what to look for and avoid. You should also seek out a local diesel mechanic to look over the vehicle and help with any repairs.

We didn't get Lolo inspected before we pulled the trigger and purchased her. We knew from the test drive that she needed new brakes and rotors, but the engine sounded good. Frankie, who is far more mechanically inclined, checked over the engine and tapped around for rust.

She was quite dirty and uncared for so we offered $4,000 even though her listing price was $6,000 and the guy jumped on it. We went to the DMV, got the paperwork sorted out and drove Lolo (very carefully) directly to a mechanic in NYC.

Because the price was so low, we figured even if it was a lemon, we could turn around and sell it to someone else willing to make the repairs and recoup our investment.

The mechanic returned with good news and bad news. He said that generally the engine was in fine working order. The bad news was that because the van was so old, there were certain parts around the engine that had exceeded their recommended lifespan of 60,000-100,000 miles (Lolo had a whopping 211,000 miles on her).

He recommended we swap out all those components and handed us a proposal with a $10,000 price tag. We took that piece of paper to AutoZone and priced out all the parts he suggested replacing at $1,600. Frankie had some, but not much experience with car engines, certainly none with diesel engines, but figured for the $8,400 in labor cost savings, he could figure it out.

We leaned on so many people during this time: neighbors with knowledge and tools; friends with an afternoon to spare; family to help with two-person jobs. We were incredibly lucky to have all this support that literally saved us thousands of dollars in labor costs. I know not everyone is in the same boat.

If you have no experience with engines and no one in your circle is able or willing to help, it's much safer to purchase a new or certified pre-owned vehicle. They will cost more at the outset, but the warranty will ensure that if anything goes wrong, you're covered by the dealership.

Even with all of Frankie's engine savvy, we've spent money on mechanics and parts along our journey. You're going to be putting a lot of miles on your van and it's going to need to be maintained. Things will breakdown and just when you think your rig is perfect, that's when something in the engine will go – pop.

You could have the mentality that you'll just drive it till it dies, cool. But then your whole home is what, just stranded who knows where? If that's your mentality, don't spend too much on your build or your rig. It would be a shame to lose all that money and hard work because you skimped on the bones or maintenance of your vehicle.

Of course, you can always pull the build out and plop it into a different van, but you might as well start with a solid foundation to avoid a huge headache down the road.

There are so many options when it comes to which vehicle to choose. Your budget will set the parameters and your personal style will make the final decision. Take all the necessary precautions to buy a vehicle with a sound engine and body structure.

Ignore the initial esthetics as a little elbow grease and some imagination can make even the ugliest vehicle a beautiful home. The engine and body structure however aren't things you can slap a coat of paint on and call it a day. These are the most important things you need to consider when choosing your vehicle.

Gathering Funds for Your Van

You're going to have to give up your daily lattes, I'm sorry. Sarcasm aside, you'll likely need to make some changes in your current lifestyle to be able to afford to build out or purchase the rig of your dreams, unless of course you have money laying around just waiting to become a composting toilet.

Once you have a rough estimate of your budget, you'll need to look at what you're currently bringing home and see if you can swing it. Some people come into van life with a set amount of money and say *I need to do it all for less than XXXX*. That's actually a great place to come at it as you won't end up over spending on things you really don't need. But it also limits your build greatly.

We originally budgeted to spend $5,000 on our entire build. As with most construction projects, we went overbudget and over schedule. All in we ended up spending $7,000.

Without that final $2,000 our van wouldn't have plumbing or walls. None of the finishing that make our space so livable would be there. When we upped the budget, we still basically just had a shell of a van.

Were we stupid when we set the original number? I don't think so. We made an educated guess based on available information.

By having this guideline, we made smart choices. Should we get the $800 diesel heater or the $150 knockoff brand? Should we get custom made window covers for $1,200 or make our own for $120? With our budget in mind, it was easy to make less expensive choices. If we didn't realize that $800 heater was a quarter of our budget, we might have splurged.

Our budget kept us in check. When we were getting close to reaching our $5,000 limit, we sat down and looked at what we still needed to buy. Since we were both still working, we had the ability to save an extra $1,000 each to complete the build the way we wanted.

By this time, we'd already gotten rid of any extraneous spending so finding the additional funds wasn't impossible. We were working 40+ hours a week and then spending every minute at home working on the van. We simply didn't have time to go out to eat or to hang out in bars. We cooked almost every meal at home because it was convenient and cheap (plus I love to cook).

We had to say no to friends who wanted to make plans because we were on such a time crunch. We couldn't give up a weekend of building for anything, we simply didn't have time (or energy) to spare which meant we didn't have time to spend on anything other than the build.

Of course, we looked at where our money was going and made a few simple changes. We cancelled any reoccurring payments we didn't need. Frankie quit two gyms he belonged to and I got rid of streaming services.

A few bucks a month adds up over time and we had the mentality that every dollar was vital to our build and the life of our dreams. Once you're really living van life, you won't need these types of services anyway, so you'll be glad you cancelled before you hit the road.

We said yes to extra work and ways to make money wherever we could. It was difficult because we didn't have much free time so those extra hours at work meant fewer hours on the build. We each had a set amount we needed to put away each month and we did whatever it took to get that money in the bank.

We had regular budget meetings and made a game of saving as much as possible. We even spent time rolling up loose change (made over $500 doing that thanks to Frankie's grandma giving us a huge jar of pennies).

Another way we earned money was by selling things we would no longer need once we moved into the van. Electronics, sports equipment, clothing, furniture, if it wasn't nailed down or for sure going in the van, we did our best to sell it. We made well over $3,000 selling a whole bunch of our old stuff. I even found a website that would buy our old books and video games by mail (made over $200 there).

Anywhere we could cut an expense or increase earnings was explored. With the budget as our guide, we easily saved every dollar we needed to fund our van life dreams. Through this process we also set our lives up to be minimalistic and cut our costs for when we would be on the road.

We learned very quickly that even when you maximize storage space in your van, you don't have room for everything you fit in your brick-and-mortar home. We are still giving goods and clothing away as we travel because as it turns out, we simply didn't need them in the first place.

Earn Free Money

Throughout the course of our build, we found several ways to earn points and free money that helped with the expense of building the van and continue to help us as we travel. Full disclosure, if you decide to sign up for these services through our links or with our promo codes, we do get a kick back. That's not why I'm recommending these services. I actually find them very useful and effective. Feel free to choose whichever services you like and leave the rest.

Fetch is an app (only in the US) that pays you for scanning receipts. After your next trip to a hardware or grocery store, simply scan your receipts and earn points. Yes, they are mining your data and give you bonus points for choosing the brands they want you to buy.

Do I care? Not really. I scanned so many receipts that weren't even my own whatever data they have on me is totally skewed. Finding receipts on the floor became just as addictive as finding coins to rollup.

Every time we went to a big box store, I would scan the parking lot for loose receipts to snap photos of. I would literally grab receipts from the top of the garbage can as I was exiting the grocery store (pre COVID of course). Once I had enough points, I would redeem them for Amazon.com gift cards – we earned well over $100 in vouchers for Amazon through Fetch. (Enter the referral code Q3WJF and we both get bonus cash for you signing up.)

Credit cards are another great way to earn free things (or a great way to get yourself into mountains of debt so watch out!). Lots of cards offer introductory bonus points you can use towards flights, cash back or hotel nights.

Generally, the deal is that you have to spend X amount of money in X number of months and pay off the card in full before you get your bonus. I decided to get two of these bonus offers, one from American Express and one from American Airlines.

The Amex card is for hotel nights which I figured would come in handy in case of van issues or crazy weather reports. If say, we came down with food poisoning or the flu, I would much rather spend two free nights in a hotel room with full plumbing and a shower than in the van.

We recently spent 2 nights for free in Las Vegas because it was going to be over 100 degrees each day and not much colder at night. After almost a year on the road, this was our first hotel and it felt so luxurious to be engulfed in fluffy white towels. Totally worth it especially since it was basically free (all you have to pay is the taxes).

The second credit card is for flight points. If we end up in a foreign land and need to fly back home asap for an emergency, I'd like to do that for free. Or if we decide we want to ship our van across the pond or store our van and go home for the holidays, we can take free flights to get to where we're going.

The third credit card we got was for Amazon.com. So many of the random items in our build weren't available anywhere except for Amazon. We were placing orders almost daily and having the rewards card really added up. Being able to apply cash back credits directly on your Amazon orders to take $5 to $100+ off each order is golden. We just redeemed a $250 credit that paid for our new Berkey water filter in full.

The last credit card we have is for Home Depot. On our first build we didn't have the card but after spending what felt like endless amounts of money there, we figured it would make sense the second time around to get the benefit of being a card holder – mainly more time to make returns which we certainly needed. At the end of our first build we had so many odds and ends left over we needed to return.

Honey is an amazing browser attachment you should have for any online shopping. It automatically tries to apply tons of coupons to your order to get you the best deal. It's free so why not try to save a few extra bucks. You're going to be spending a fair amount of money on your build and shopping online. Make all these purchases count as points or cash back so that you can benefit from your spending and if you can use a coupon code to spend a little less, awesome.

The final way to earn free money is to find second hand or free building supplies. You can scan online market places to buy used items like sinks, wood and paint. Building supplies are expensive so any freebies or cheap pieces will make your build more affordable. Lookout at the side of the road for discarded furniture or décor items.

Visit Habitat for Humanity ReStore or second-hand stores for awesome finds. Of course, you can buy new everything but we found that used items were usually pretty high quality at a third of the price (or free!).

Throughout this whole process we really had to examine our relationship with money. No coin was too small, no discount too insignificant. If I could get a 3% coupon code or a $5 gift certificate, I was using it. We brought recycling back to the depot for coins. A family member gave us their bucket of pennies and we spent hours rolling them up.

There is no shame in my budget game. Building a van is not cheap no matter how many discounts you can accumulate, but it would be much more expensive if you didn't try.

As much time and energy we put towards saving, we also had to be comfortable spending. The ebb and flow of money is that you have to be equally as happy to save as you are to spend.

When we went from saving to spending, I had a hard time letting go. This caused friction and made the process less enjoyable. Once I realized that money is just a tool, it is limitless and flows freely and easily, I had a much easier time spending where needed.

Frankie and I have done a lot of work and reading on our money mindset which has helped tremendously with this lifestyle. Rather than hoarding our money, not wanting to spend on anything and fussing over every cent, we spend where we need to, give where we feel compelled, and accept graciously when money is given to us.

If you want to expand your views on money The Secret is an amazing book and movie on Netflix to get you started or read anything on the law of attraction.

Enough about money, let's get our hands dirty.

The Build

Nothing is level and nothing is square. This is the number one rule of van builds. Your van is likely not a box (unless you got a box truck) - it's wider on the bottom than it is on the top. That means your beautiful bench seat will need a 15-inch piece of wood at the base and a 13 5/8th piece at the top.

Don't even get me started about upper cabinets – they are so tricky. Every single piece of furniture that is built in your van will be completely custom. Get used to measuring 3 times, cutting once, putting it in, realizing it doesn't fit, cutting it again and then finally saying screw it it's good enough.

If you are not blessed to have carpentry, electrical, plumbing or other special talents that will come in handy, it's time to step up. If I can wield a table saw and wire a stereo, there's nothing you can't do.

Of course, we had help from friends and family but I'll tell you what, likely no one will be as helpful as they said they would be or you thought they might be.

Building a van requires hours and weeks of hard labor. Sure, people will pop in and help, but you should never rely too heavily on them unless you are paying them. We learned this the hard way after being let down one too many times.

The best part of building your own van is the satisfaction that comes with knowing you created it. It might not be perfect, you might break a nail, get a splinter, or drop a hammer on your foot, but *you* built it. It's all yours chicken little, every imperfection is like a thumbprint.

That's not to say that there's any less pride or satisfaction in having someone else build it for you. Lots of people hire specialists to help with certain aspects of their build or to build the whole thing. Something to keep in mind is that a house plumber has never plumed a van. An electrician has likely never set up a mini solar system.

Our friends had their tiny home plumbed by a house plumber and are losing gallons of water daily from the hot water heater pressure valve because it was set up for a house not for a van. You have to consider that the heat from the engine that is heating the water is super high which sets off the pressure valve every time they drive. This wouldn't even be a consideration in a house build.

There are also companies who will do all the work for you. You drop off your empty van and they return a complete tiny home on wheels. This is great for people who don't want to or don't have time to build their own rigs. But this does come with a hefty price tag. The cheapest professional build outfit I've seen listed their prices starting at $20,000 (you bring the van). We've toured rigs that came with $100,000 price tags. It's wild out there.

It took us six months to build our first rig. As I've said, we were both working full time so we only had evenings and weekends available.

Depending on the complexity of your build and the number of dedicated hours you have to spend on it, build times will vary greatly. I've seen builds completed in a month and I've seen people who spend years tinkering, adding and completing one project at a time as money and motivation become available. Just like with your budget, you can reverse engineer your build.

If you know you want to be on the road in X number of months, how many days do you have to complete each project?

You'll read in the next few chapters about options for each component of your build: electrical, plumbing, insulation, heat, and finally layout. Once you've decided on these, you can start to plan for your very basic, or very complex systems and build requirements.

Again, before you can get to any of these items, step one in any build is laying a strong foundation. You spent so much time finding a rig that had good bones and engine structure. Now you get to reinforce and solidify these elements.

Completing a good once over of the engine, replacing any worn-out parts and dealing with any mechanical issues comes first. If you're worried too much tinkering in the engine might unearth a ghastly problem, just remember how glad you'll be to find it now, not when stranded on the road somewhere.

This also means making sure you've got heavy duty tires with lots of tread. You do not want to be driving your 5000 plus pound home on bald tires.

Next up, you want to deal with any rust, holes, or structural issues. If you bought an RV knowing it needed a new roof, do that first. If you have holes in your floor that have been eaten out by rust, you need to clean and patch those with fiberglass.

Foundation first, do not skip this step, or you will regret it later. We spent the first month and a half of our first build cleaning, repairing rust, swapping out engine parts and dreaming about the day when we could actually build the interior.

This is also the time to cut holes in your vehicle's body. We cut two big holes in the roof for our two MaxxAir Fans. If you are going to add a window, AC unit, skylight, exhaust fan or port hole, do it now. This is also when we installed our solar system on the roof which involved lots of drilling into the body of our van (to avoid all the holes mount everything to a roof rack).

By installing these first, you can ensure they're not going to leak before you put up walls and other expensive finishing. Make sure you FULLY clean up any metal shards from cutting, they will immediately create rust on anything they touch - learned that the hard way.

One of the biggest regrets I hear from people who've built out theirs van is that they wish they did it in a different order.

Sometimes you'll realize you have to take down a project you've already spent time on because something else needs to go behind it or you realize you were supposed to do something else first. Learning from our own mistakes, here's the order we suggest you build in.

First up is electrical. Once your solar is mounted on the roof and you've ensured you have no leaks, you'll want to run your wiring. Of course, in order to do this, you'll need to have a good idea of your layout. Where are you going to need outlets, switches, water pumps, water heaters, lights and any other hard-wired electrical components?

If you don't have at least a working draft of your layout, you won't know where to run your lines. If you decide to run your lines after you frame the build, you will have to snake the wires around the frame or have the wires completely outside the wall (you can buy casing for this).

The cleanest look however, is wired behind the walls/ceiling/floor which means it needs to go in first. Once everything is run, install the switches and lights and plugs just to make sure they work properly. Once we knew everything was run correctly, we took off all those final pieces and taped up the end of the wires. That way the walls and ceiling could be mounted, cords pulled through and then switches and plugs were reattached outside the finished walls.

Next up is framing and insulation. Framing turns your metal box into something you can actually build off of. Beams should be no more than 12 to 16 inches apart on the floor and a max of 24 inches on the walls and ceiling.

A beam is basically a long piece of wood, generally a 2x3 or 2x4 that you drill into the metal of your vehicle so that you can mount your wall and other furnishings to it. Think about if you've ever had to find studs (beams) in your wall at home to mount a TV or hang something else heavy. You typically would use a stud finder to locate these beams because they are the sturdiest part of the wall. Same goes for your van build.

You can forgo framing by drilling your wall directly into the vans metal beams, but you give up a whole lot of insulation which decreases the efficiency of your heating and cooling efforts. Most vans have metal frames that you will be securing the wood beams to. In theory, you could mount your finished wall to the metal frame and just insulate behind that.

If you go that route, you will need to keep very good track of where those metal frames are (because they won't be even squares, evenly spaced, or even the same on each side) and plan your layout around those.

You can't hang an upper cabinet on a piece of plywood with no frame or beam behind it because it will eventually come crashing down - ouch.

On the flip side you want to make sure that your beams aren't so wide that they are taking away valuable living space. You only have so many inches to work with, so any additional space savings are a blessing. We went with 2x3s but laid them so that the wide part was flush with the wall and the 2-inch side was all that was sticking out. After insulating around those, we felt we had maximized the insulation to framing ratio.

You can also look into sound deadening pads for the metal to take away tons of road noise from the frame of the van. This can be expensive if you try to cover every single metal surface of your van but you really don't have to. Some is better than none so even if you only buy one case, that's cool. For our second build we got 4 boxes of the knock off stuff and covered like 80% of the rig focusing on the wheel wells and floor - it works great.

Now you can lay your floor over the beams, insulation, sound deadening and wiring you've already laid down.

Most people go with a floating laminate or vinyl "wood" floor because they are easy to install and are suitable for rugged living.

Be sure to choose waterproof board with attached underlayment so you don't have to lay down a separate layer of this yourself. This saves you time, money and effort.

I can't even explain to you how happy I was when we were finally finished laying down the floor. After weeks of back breaking labor, this was the first real visual sign that we were building a beautiful home.

You would think the next step would be to put up your walls but it's actually the ceiling. By putting up your walls last, they sandwich between the floor and ceiling, supporting them and keeping them in place. For the ceiling, you might have to cut out holes for fans and lighting.

You'll need to pull the wiring through if you're doing pot or overhead lights. For this job it's really useful to have multiple hands on deck because it's very tricky to hold up a huge piece of wood (or even a small piece of wood), get it in the right place and screw it in all by yourself.

After the ceiling is up you move on to your walls. Be sure that you cut openings for your outlets and switches and that you create a snug fit between the ceiling and floor. For all our walls and ceilings, we first put up a layer of plywood as our base and then installed finished product on top of this.

For the floor this is required because the floating floor needs a sturdy base. For the ceiling and walls, you can choose to use either better quality plywood, Masonite, wood slats or other sturdy finished product and forgo the plywood. By doing this you save the ¼ inch on each side and save yourself the step of adding essentially a second wall.

Depending on how intense your plumbing system is going to be (we'll discuss this shortly), you might not have to build anything. If you want a system more similar to what you have in a house, you'll have to mount your tanks, run piping, install switches, filters, traps, elbow joints, kill switches, pressure valves and the like.

You won't be able to mount your sink until your cabinetry is finished but you should have a clear understanding of where everything is going to be and have it roughly laid out so you can build cabinetry to accommodate your system.

If you're going for a more basic set up, make sure there is enough storage space for fresh and grey water tanks under the sink or wherever you plan on running the lines. If you're going to mount your tanks outside the vehicle, you'll have to drill more holes through your floor or walls.

Cabinetry is another area of the build where you can either go incredibly detailed or very basic. I've seen a few "master carpenter" van builds and holy cow they are spectacular! The detail, the workmanship, who knew wood could look like that?

Most of us do not have the skills or the money to pay for them. You'll likely have to settle for something less grand. Basic doesn't have to be boring though. Of course, functionality comes first, but you can always jazz up your cabinet faces with a splash of paint, vintage knobs, or interesting live-edge wood.

When it comes to cabinetry, you must also consider that your home is going to move around a lot. You don't want doors swinging open and drawers slamming shut every time you take a turn. Trust me it's no fun cleaning up the mess afterwards.

Safety first guys. Make sure all your cabinets, cupboards, drawers, shelves and the like are securely mounted to the walls and that their doors/drawers are secured with magnets or other locking mechanisms.

What cabinets you need will depend on how you want to layout your build. We went with a large kitchen area with lots of storage underneath, a multi-purpose couch/storage area, a standing desk that doubles as shelving storage, a tall bedside table with hanging storage underneath (hanging storage is useless, don't bother, we've already repurposed this area with a ring of hooks instead), and finally one large upper cabinet because building a second one would have taken away all of our sanity.

You think you need tons of storage and in a sense, you do, but you also don't need so much storage that your whole build is basically one nook after the next filled with more junk. We're supposed to be downsizing, remember?!

Finally, you can move onto finishing touches like tile/wall paper/painting, knobs, handles, hooks. This also includes finishing up plumbing and electrical systems if there was anything you missed on those.

To reiterate, in my opinion, from my experience and the gathered experience of others, I would suggest building your van in this order:

1. Foundation: engine, rust, body structure
2. Cut Big Holes: fans, skylight, windows, etc.
3. Check for Leaks During Crazy Rain Storms
4. Electrical: solar and wiring
5. Framing and Insulating

6. Floor
7. Ceiling
8. Walls
9. Plumbing; big pieces and layout of pipes
10. Cabinets
11. Finishing Touches

Allow me to note that there is always more than one way to achieve your desired goals. This is basic build methodology. There are many other ways to build a van.

You can use metal beams or 80/20 instead of wood ones, you can buy everything from Ikea and fit it in, and you can go in any order you like. I'm laying out the most common way for you to do it, a way I know will work.

If you want to research, forge a path and build it your own way, by all means, please do. Then write me a note to let me know all about it! Right now, we are working through our second build and vlogging the whole process. Like giving birth, you forget how painful it is when you see your beautiful baby.

We loved living in Lolo and when the opportunity arose to sell her and start over, we jumped on it. Now that we are building, I am left wondering, *"what the heck were we thinking?"!* Soon enough we will be back on the road enjoying all that van life has to offer - is what I keep reminding myself so as not to lose my mind.

"Each of us is carving a stone, erecting a column, or cutting a piece of stained glass in the construction of something much bigger than ourselves." — Adrienne Clarkson

Big Mistakes to Avoid in Your Build

There are a few great big mistakes you will want to avoid when building out your van. I've gathered these errors from my own experience and from the experiences of others. It's one thing if you wish you put your kitchen in the front instead of the back, or that you'd painted green instead of blue. It's another to end up with a huge leak or fire or another disastrous event that could have been avoided.

Way back when you were shopping for a van, you checked for leaks. Before you insulate or put up any walls, you want to make damn sure you don't have any. If you noticed water marks or rust stains at seams or windows, investigate. We used a strong silicone waterproof caulking at all junctures of metal to metal.

We also used fiberglass on bigger holes or weaker, more damaged, junctures. After making any holes in the body (for vents, windows, drains, or screws) we silicone sealed them like crazy. When we were done sealing holes, we hosed down the van and checked for leaks. We didn't have any – hooray!

A few days later, there was a torrential downpour. We went and sat in the van during the storm and identified multiple locations that needed additional patching.

The last thing you want is to discover a water leak *after* you've put up walls and fancy lights. To mitigate the damage, you'll have to tear down all your hard work and make a great big mess.

Either that or you live with the mold and mildew building in behind your walls – or just move to the desert! This is not an issue you want to have so do everything you can to avoid it.

Next, think for a moment, what will happen if you get into a car accident? If you smash into something, will that giant cabinet in the back of your build become a projectile? Safety is number one when building your van. Everything needs to be tightly secured to very strong and stable walls, the ceiling and or floor (or all three).

If you've got more than two people in your van, you need to have legal seats and seatbelts for everyone. I've seen firsthand how destructive an open cabinet can be when you take a turn too hard - every jar and dish is smashed all over the floor.

I've seen images of van life vans that have been in wrecks and it's not pretty. Please, I implore you, secure everything including all cabinet doors and always wear your seatbelt. Don't be a fool, even Kanye wasn't too cool for the safe belt.

Explosive gasses are one of the most dangerous things you'll have on board. When you are building a traditional home, there are codes you must adhere to for things like propane. In a van, no one is checking in on you making sure you've done it right.

We met a couple who have an entire propane system set up in their van for heat and cooking. As soon as people their van tour on our YouTube channel, I got flooded with comments about how unsafe their propane system is, how the tanks are improperly stored, how they are a disaster waiting to happen.

I pray to all things holy that they never have any issues. I pray that you never have any issues. I pray that you do your research and figure out the safest way to set up any dangerous systems and take all the precautions to make sure you're protected even if it costs a few extra dollars.

When building your bed frame, make sure your mattress can breathe. If you put your mattress on a single sheet of wood with no holes in it, it's going to grow mold and get nasty under there. I've seen it so many times, don't make this mistake. Use bed slats or drill swiss cheese style holes all over the wood.

If you're cutting any holes into the metal structure of the van, make sure you not only seal these holes with a waterproof adhesive but also that you clean away any metal fragments left behind.

After we cut our roof holes and installed our fans, we congratulated ourselves with a job well done and went in for the night - what turned out to be a very rainy night. The next day when we came out to check for leaks, we noticed that the whole roof was covered in a layer of rust.

All those metal fragments had oxidized during the rainstorm and now we had rust dots everywhere. We had to clean this all up and repaint our whole roof with rust resistant paint. Not recommended and best avoided.

Many vanlifers regret the amount of money they spent on labor during their build. Most of us come into this lifestyle with little to no knowledge of mechanical, plumbing, electrical, carpentry and the like. We think ourselves incapable of completing these projects and outsource the work. While this is great there are a few pitfalls.

First, most builders and plumbers have never worked on a van. There are intricacies involved in van systems that are not the same as with house systems. Often these pros will be doing the same research you could be doing on how to set up your solar system or on demand hot water heater. Sure, they have years of background on the topic, but I've heard many vanlifers complain that the people doing their work were just as clueless as they were. By doing the research and work yourself, you know that it's van specific.

Plus hiring out work is going to cost an arm and a leg. Many professionals charge upwards of $100 an hour which will rack up fast. Sometimes the biggest expense for a build, is the labor cost that went into it – that's why professional builds cost so much.

We have a few van life friends who make their living by building other people's vans (@aimlesstravels). I would wholeheartedly trust these guys to build my van because they've done it so many times and know the intricacies of van specific builds. They're who we call when we have a question on our own build.

No matter who you hire, by doing the majority or all of the work yourself, you save thousands of dollars. The more experience you have with a table saw or plumbing system, the more knowledgeable you'll become with it. At the end of the day, you'll feel a massive sense of accomplishment with what you've built.

We have friends who started off my paying others to do the work, ran out of money, and had to finish everything themselves. We have friends who started with zero experience and built beautiful vans with no help at all. It is possible to do all the work yourself, believe you can do it!

I'm sure there are other pitfalls not mentioned and every build has its *"I wish I had done that differently"* moments. Don't worry though, with a little bit of research and effort, there's nothing you can't accomplish.

Electrical

When it comes to powering your build, don't be like me and get completely overwhelmed then totally give up. According to Frankie electrical systems are actually quite straight forward, but of course not like in a house. Sure, you can just plug your laptop into an outlet but only if you have an inverter to convert the solar power you're bringing in to 120-volts. Yes, you can charge your cell phone in a USB port as long as your 12-volt system is up and running.

Most vans have two electrical systems powered by one or two methods. When the solar comes in from the roof, it passes through the panels, into the charge controller which converts that energy into the power needed to charge your batteries. From the batteries directly, depending on the voltage you purchased (12 is the most common but they also come in 6 and 24) you can directly power your 12-volt system.

We have our fans, fridge, water pump, USB charger, and lights running directly on this 12-volt system. The benefit of this system is that you don't have to convert the power again to use it.

Converting the power from your batteries to 120-volts, the power needed for standard electrical outlets, requires more power and additional components. You will need an inverter that takes the 12-volt power and turns it into 120-volt power.

Generally, the 120 system will be on a switch. When you want the outlets to work, you switch on your inverter. When you don't need the outlets, you turn the inverter off to conserve power. That's because things that run on outlets tend to draw a lot more energy. The more you can have on your 12-volt system the better. We also have extra controls and switches for things on the 120 system so that when we turn it on, everything doesn't try to turn on all at once and fry our batteries.

Because the 120 system takes significantly more power than the 12-volt system you'll want to have your bigger items like the fridge on the 12-volt system so you don't constantly have to have your inverter on.

If you can set your 12-volt system up with a number of USB ports you can pretty much charge all your electronics without issue. I often hear vanlifers talk about how their inverters scream at them (go into default) when they are doing simple tasks because there's not enough power in the system.

For that reason alone, you want to make sure you can live without anything on the 120 system - winter is coming, you won't always have a full charge.

When shopping for appliances, plugs, USB chargers and the like, simply add the words 12-volt to your search parameters and you'll see there are many options.

We've seen builds where they have practically everything running on the 12-volt system and rarely turn on the inverter. We've seen builds where they try to keep as much off the solar system as possible, hanging battery operated lights, choosing no power foot pumps for their water systems and only using solar to charge their phones.

I've also seen builds with zero solar. They use a battery-to-battery charger to power their systems. By that I mean, when the van engine is running, the alternator (car battery charger) sends power to the house batteries in the back through a solenoid or DC to DC charger.

We had a simple solenoid on a switch in Lolo, but you can also buy a trickle charger designed specifically for this purpose. For most vanifers the battery-to-battery charger is a backup device.

On cloudy days or if we have a long drive with little sunshine, we'll flip the switch and charge the batteries. Before we had this system set up, we often ran out of juice and had to severely limit our electricity consumption until we found some sunshine.

You also have two main choices for batteries to store all this sunshine and car generated power. The ultimate choice is lithium-ion batteries. These are lightweight, small in size and can be drained 100% without any damage to the battery. The downside is that one of these batteries' costs over $1000.

For our first build we went with the second, less expensive option of deep cycle AMG batteries. These are bigger and bulkier, weighing 60-80 pounds each (a lithium battery weighs about 20 pounds). For our second build we found lithium batteries for less than $600 each and with 5% back on our Amazon credit card, they were a steal!

The biggest downside of AMG is that to avoid damaging the longevity of the battery, you can't drain it below 50%. That means you will need 2 AMG batteries to do the work of 1 lithium battery. It also means you need to be more aware of where your battery levels are sitting so that you don't accidently drain your system. But with each AMG battery costing only about $100, even if you have to buy 5, you've still saved money (but certainly not weight).

Then it's just the matter of putting it all together. Mounting the solar panels to the roof, connecting them to each other then down to the charge controller, into the battery, out to the inverter and 12-volt system. Easy-peasy right?! Frankie is the real expert on this subject and is happy to talk you through the process (of this or any other technical aspect of your build). Feel free to reach out to him on Instagram or via our website (www.fnavanlife.com) to book a call or chat online.

"You can design and create, and build the most wonderful place in the world. But it takes people to make the dream a reality."
— Walt Disney

Insulation and Heat

Some vanlifers argue that because they plan on only being in temperate climates, they don't need to insulate. This is moronic. Insulation doesn't just stop you from being cold, it also stops you from being too hot. Also, those hot desert days quickly turn into freezing nights.

Our climate is becoming more and more erratic. You might think you're going to have a lovely day but then a snowstorm rolls in. Are you really going to be monitoring the weather that closely?

One night in New Hampshire, we had been talking to a local who mentioned that it was going to be floating around freezing that night. We cozied up in bed with our diesel heater on set to low. When we woke up at 3am freezing and could see our breath, we realized the temperature was way colder outside than anticipated. Turns out it was -7 degrees Fahrenheit (that's -21 Celsius).

If we hadn't been properly insulated and had a heater ready to blast hot air as soon as we realized our mistake, we would have been frozen!

There are a few different ways to insulate your van. Depending on your environmental tendencies, some of these will be more appealing than others.

The least expensive is foam board insulation. Well, that might not actually be true as I've seen vans with some pretty shitty insulation choices (AstroTurf?!) so I'll rephrase to note this is the least expensive actual insulation product.

We used foam board in our first build, each sheet (depending on the thickness) cost about $20 and we needed approximately 6 sheets. This method is cheap but also labor intensive. Unlike the wall of a house, you do not have a large flat surface for the board to sit in. For a van, foam board is not easy to work with, it's annoying to cut and jam into places. It took a good amount of time to fully insulate our van but it was well worth the struggle. Lolo is very well insulated and I wouldn't trade that for anything.

Next up are stuffing like wool and loose fill insulation materials. These are eco-friendlier (not if you're vegan) but more costly as well. I've seen full vans done using these and they make it very easy to get into all the nooks and crannies. We're going with Havelock Wool for van build number two so we'll let you know the difference.

You can also get spray insulation, but this either needs to be done by a professional or if you are going to buy a kit and do it yourself, you need to tarp down anything within a 5-foot radius of the van that you don't want spray foam on.

Friends of ours did this and they said it was nearly impossible to get the foam exactly where you wanted it and they were cleaning it off the exterior of their freshly painted van for ages. They however choose a very eco-friendly spray foam which was their biggest concern.

If you want to go very budget minded and aren't planning on going anywhere too cold, you can use heavy duty moving blankets from companies like Harbor Freight. Or just use large amounts of silver sheets of bubble wrap, Reflectix.

Reflectix also act as a vapor barrier in your van. That means that it helps to prevent the growth of mold behind your walls. In a house, a vapor barrier is very important, but there's some debate in the van community whether a vapor barrier actually works the same way as it does in a house.

Since a van isn't completely sealed, the vapor barrier can't do all that it's intended to do. For us it was an extra layer of insulation and we figured as that's how builders have been doing it for decades, there must be some logic to it.

Now that you've got a way to keep the heat in, it's time to start the fire (which is actually a legitimate option for some builds). The easiest way to get heat into a van (other than running the engine heat) is a built-in heater. Some run on propane, some on gasoline, some on diesel. Ours is tapped right into the diesel tank for the entire vehicle so we know that if there's fuel in the car, we can keep ourselves warm.

Most fuel pumps on the main gas tank for the vehicle have what's called an auxiliary port that you can easily hook the heater into. If you don't want to tap your vans fuel line, you can use a secondary tank with the fuel in it or get a propane system.

The other option with propane is the little Mr. Heaters. These are very effective at heating small spaces but also pose a fire risk so be sure to shut it off before bed and keep it away from any pets (or clumsy elbows).

School buses and RVs come with preexisting insulation. For the RVs this is likely sufficient and beyond checking for mold and sealing drafty spots, you'll probably not have to do much else. School buses also have some insulation, after all they are designed to keep kids safe and warm.

But that insulation is generally lacking and counts on there being 30 bodies in the bus all generating heat plus having a heater pumping. As a Canadian kid, I remember getting on the bus early in the morning. We were the first stop so no one else was on the bus when we got on. It was frosty! It wasn't until we had picked up about 20 other kids that I was finally able to unzip my winter coat.

Windows and doors also need to be considered when you're thinking about insulation. You're going to lose a lot of heat in the winter and take in a ton of heat in the summer if you don't have appropriate window coverings.

You can purchase custom window coverings for your van online but these run about $1,000 for a complete set. We made our own out of Reflectix and fabric for about $100. I custom made them to fit our two back windows, large side window and the entire front cab.

In the winter these have saved us by keeping the heat from our diesel heater inside the van and in the summer, they help keep the sun and its blazing heat out to keep us nice and cool.

In the summer our great big sliding door is amazing for creating a nice cross breeze. In the winter though, that door sucks out all the heat from the van. We do our absolute best to only use the front cab doors in the winter because of it.

The back doors are also heat drainers in the winter. We really needed to get a set of curtains up there so that Frankie could access his tools in the back and I can stay warm in the front. Speaking of curtains, we have a set that separate our front cab and living area. These not only regulate hot and cold but also keep out any prying eyes giving us more privacy.

Your home is a giant metal box. Metal is not good at regulating temperature at all, when it's hot outside metal is hot, when it's cold, metal is cold. If you don't have that layer of insulation, you'll find yourself at the whim of mother nature more often than you'd like.

Plumbing

Just like with electrical, plumbing comes in all ranges from very basic to super high tech. At the end of the day, all you need is clean water to wash your dishes and clean your face. Bonuses like showers and flushing toilets require a lot more thought.

Something I didn't realize when we ventured into van life was that water on board has 3 different classifications. First you have fresh water, this is obvious. Next you have grey water, this is water that's been used to clean dishes or shower with. Third you have black water; this is water that you've gone to the bathroom in. Our rig only has fresh and grey water tanks because we have a very simple toilet system that doesn't require storing any wastewater.

Let's talk toilets. We've legit got a bucket to number 2 in and a funnel to number 1 in. This system probably cost us $20 in total. I know people who've paid over $1000 for their toilet system. To us it just wasn't worth it.

When you're in the city, you can always find a coffee shop or other location to use the bathroom. When you're in the wilderness, you can always dig a hole. Don't worry, we've got a whole section dedicated to where to go to the bathroom coming up.

But I will say, now that we are looking to build a second rig, we're definitely going to have a composting toilet onboard. Mainly for emergencies but now that we're not quite so worried about budget, we're willing to splurge a little bit to poop on a toilet rather than in a plastic bag (not glamorous).

Everyone loves a good shower. I love a good bath even more but the likelihood of me getting a full bathtub in a van is pretty low, sadly. When designing our build, we seriously considered having a shower. Being able to shower whenever you want is a luxury most people in the developed world have grown accustomed to. Could we really live without showering for days?

The biggest drawback for us when it came to a shower was the amount of space we would have to dedicate to it. From all the van tours we were seeing, most people used their showers for storage and rarely for actual showers.

If you do want to build a shower, you must make sure the area is completely watertight including any lighting you install in there (and you'll need a light in there unless you want to shower in the dark or add a window/skylight).

You'll also need to think about drainage as you'll have to pipe the grey water into your grey water tank or directly to the earth which is a tricky conundrum that environmentalists wouldn't love. Steam should also be a consideration as you don't want moisture accumulating in your van. Many people put fans above their showers to alleviate this issue.

For an adequate shower you need a powerful water pump to supply enough water, a water tank big enough to hold enough water and a very low-flow shower faucet so that you don't burn through all that water you're storing in 3 minutes. Showers are tricky business and there are a lot of places to shower on the road so you'll need to think about if you want to dedicate the time, energy, space, and water into building a shower on board. More on this later.

The most important plumbing aspect of any build is the sink. That's because the kitchen sink is also the bathroom sink. It's where you will do dishes and wash your face. The sink in your build is going to get a workout everyday so this is where you want to make sure you get exactly what you need.

The simplest set up is to have a gravity do all the work for you. This involves having a jug at sink level or higher that, when the faucet is opened, will pour water into your sink.

The next simplest set up would be to have that same jug below the sink and use a foot pump to move the water from the floor up to the faucet in the sink. Jugs for this set up are usually quite small (relatively speaking) so that you can pick them up and carry them to be filled. If they are too big, you'll struggle to carry the full jugs back to the van.

Next up you can have a system with big tanks in the back that will require a water pump to pump the water to the front of your build. This system is much more complicated. Because it's pressurized, there's a real likelihood that you can over pressurize and end up with a leak. But as long as all your piping and fittings are rated for the correct PSI, you're good.

No matter what system you choose, you're going to end up with two to three different tanks, fresh, grey and black. Some people choose to house some or all of their tanks outside/under their van and piped in. Often, they are housed under the van near the back tires or along the sides.

First you have to make sure that you still have adequate clearance since you don't want to knock your tank loose every time you go over a speed bump. The next thing to consider is that in cold weather, this tank can freeze and then you won't be able to empty it. When your pipes and tanks freeze, they expand which means your system can get majorly damaged.

We've had our pipes freeze up on us twice and our whole system is indoors. The pipes are located right near the back doors under the bed and because this area isn't well heated, it gets pretty cold down there. Both times, we were without plumbing for days and then were forced to replace damaged elements of our plumbing system after everything thawed. Not fun.

We've since added a heat trace to our pipes and tanks that's basically a heated power cord that gets hot when it senses it's cold out. A perfect low-cost solution that does eat up a lot of power.

A more expensive but very nifty solution is to pipe your engine coolant from your engine into radiant heat lines all over your van. This allows you to keep your water system warm and heat your floors in the middle of the winter. This was on my wish list for our next build but quickly got the axe when we realized the cost of such a system as well as the, albeit slim, chance the lines might leak and your whole build would be floating on a sea of glycol.

In any case you've got to think about cold temperatures when building out your plumbing system. If you're going to just have a few tanks under your cabinets, those will be easier to keep above freezing and even if they do freeze, they won't create a whole host of issues when they thaw.

A few more things to think about, your faucet might look pretty, but does it use way too much water? For both the shower system and the sink, you'll want to make sure you're getting a low flow faucet so you don't blow through your water in a day.

Over time you'll get used to how much water you're actually using and develop ways to use less.

This isn't something we really think about when we live in homes because water is generally free flowing. It doesn't matter how long your showers are or how you wash your dishes because the water doesn't ever run out.

After living in a van for a while, you'll start to conserve as much as possible so you need to fill up as little as possible. Or at least, that's how we roll.

Filling up water is really not that hard or complicated. On apps like iOverlander you can ask to see locations for water fill ups. Many gas stations have hookups as do RV parks, national parks and if you're ever staying with friends or family, their house most certainly has a hose. For smaller jugs you can carry, lots of grocery stores have water fill stations where you pay by the gallon. There's always somewhere to fill up so don't worry about it.

Plumbing is another one of those intimidating van build tasks but with a little preplanning you'll be good to go. If you're unsure, keep the system simple. If you want all the bells and whistles, make sure you do it right. While we were so concerned about water leaking in from the roof, just imagine how bad it would be if all your plumbing lines were leaking!

"The whole difference between construction and creation is exactly this: that a thing constructed can only be loved after it is constructed; but a thing created is loved before it exists." — Charles Dickens

Layout

To be totally honest, I didn't care that much about the technical components of the build. All I cared about was how it was going to look! This frustrated Frankie to no end. I would be asking him about colors and fabric while he was researching electrical setups.

I couldn't wait to get to the point of our build where I could choose backsplashes and flooring and throw pillows – oh my! Frankie kept pushing me off and sanely pointing out that without walls and cabinetry, my fruit hammock would have nowhere to hang. But the layout, this was something he was onboard to figure out with me from the get go.

We spent countless hours watching van tours on YouTube. We watched tours featuring all different kinds of vehicles with all different budgets. Each tour either showed me something I really wanted or something I really didn't want.

I could see what it was like for the people to move around in their space, how much storage they had, how easy it was for them to cook, shower and live.

I kept a list of all the things I wanted - this list was very, very long. Looking back at it now, we actually have only about half of the items on my wish list and that's okay. The point is to start dreaming and visualizing yourself in the space.

One great way to do this is to map out your floor plan in life size. We used blue painters' tape on the floor of our apartment to lay out the exact dimensions of our van sized living space. Then we experimented with different layouts. How much space would we save by having a full-sized bed instead of a queen? How deep should our cabinets be? How much walking space would we have if we extended the couch 2 inches? Would my yoga mat still fit on the floor?

Being able to move the tape around into different configurations and then playing house - walking from the fridge to the bed etc. allowed us to feel what it would be like living in the layout we were testing. We practiced what it would be like to walk past each other and laid down in our bed to see if it was long enough.

Once the whole thing was mapped out on the floor the way we wanted it, we took that layout to pen and paper to flush out the design.

There are apps and websites where you can design your layout and layouts of popular builds for sale online. You can certainly use these services to help you imagine your build or to get a fully flushed out layout from your favorite build. A paint by numbers guide if you will.

This is a great way to support channels you love, gather ideas and see what you might need in terms of building materials. We didn't use any of these services ourselves. Frankie tinkered with a free program for a while but found it frustrating and gave up.

We did our whole build pen on paper and then when we actually went to build it, we followed that guide the best we could. So many of the measurements and dimensions you have on paper will be useless in the actual van. Curved walls and uneven everything will require you to measure and cut every piece of wood customized to your van.

Our best advice is to build from the back to the front of the van. For our layout, the most important aspect was having our bed high enough and long enough so that our bikes and snowboards could fit in the "garage" underneath.

Because of this, the first thing we built was our bed frame. Once this was in place, we could take specific measurements for how long the kitchen could be. If we started with the kitchen, we might have ended up with the wrong amount of space for our garage.

A few lessons we learned after living in our van is that hanging storage is stupid, taking out a cooktop every meal is annoying but manageable, and even with a few imperfections, we're still so incredibly happy with our build and layout. That's because we designed it specifically for ourselves!

We knew that being able to roll out a yoga mat on the floor was a must, that having lots of space to cook was nonnegotiable, that having a ton of storage for all our outdoor adventure gear was vital. We knew what kind of travels we wanted to do and what kind of people we are.

This informed our whole layout. Your layout will be as unique as you are. It should reflect your lifestyle, the activities and comforts that are important to you. If you build your home with your dreams in mind, you'll never regret the choices you make.

I'm not going to sugar coat it, building a van is a ton of hard work. As we move through our second build, we are yet again faced with long days of hard labor and evenings spent thinking and planning for the next days tasks. I'm having stress dreams about framing and electrical. My whole body aches. Frankie and I are getting cross with each other more often. We're both tired and hungry and over worked.

Sure, we could slow down and take the build at a leisurely pace but if you're anything like us you'll know that we just want to get back on the road already.

Once we're finished and living on the road all the aches and pains of building will be like dust rolling off the back of the van. Perseverance is absolutely a required attribute to completing your very own van build, but if you can weather the storm, a beautiful life awaits.

"When you're traveling, you are what you are, right there and then. People don't have your past to hold against you. No yesterdays on the road." — William Least Heat-Moon

Leaving Your Life Behind

This was one of the biggest surprises for me. After spending so much time planning and building, when we gave our landlord the keys to our apartment and drove away, I was in shock. I expected elation, joy, excitement. I encountered fear, anxiety, worry, and numbness.

Had I just quit my job and sold everything I owned to move into a glorified RV? I had been so on board with the process that when the results arrived, I didn't know what to do or how to feel.

If you're a weekend warrior (someone who lives van life on the weekends or enjoys extended road trips) you'll likely never experience these feelings. The grieving for your old life, unsure of what the future holds. That leap into the unknown is scary even if you're excited for it.

The next time you come back to this place, you'll be a changed person and that place you called home will never be the same.

It took me a few weeks to get settled into life on the road. I was constantly stressed out, worried about where we were going to sleep, fretting about how we were going to find cheap gas, feeling self-conscious about driving our big rig into small towns and generally figuring out how to live in this tiny space.

Although I was having fun every day and enjoying the views and scenery we were experiencing, it was tough. I struggled mentally and emotionally to find my footing in this new way of life. I was lucky to have a supportive partner to help ease my worries. Frankie was the only person in the world who could really understand what I was going through. I leaned on him to be brave and bold for both of us.

Eventually, I settled in. I found new routines, created structure in our ever-changing scenery. I got more comfortable cooking and sleeping. I felt like I knew my way around our home. I started to enjoy each new town and every new adventure rather than worrying about things out of my control.

Nowadays there's nowhere I would rather be than on the road. When I stay put for too long, I start to crave the adventure. I look at photos of mountains we could be climbing or hot springs we could be soaking in and I want to pack up and go. I no longer worry about where we're going to sleep or get food or find water or what people think about our rig, because everything always works itself out.

Moving into the van and facing my fears has been a game changer for my anxiety. Before we left New York, I was stressed out and having almost daily panic attacks. My subway ride into work was terrifying because I didn't know if I was going to have to frantically exit the train halfway to my destination because my heart was beating so hard I thought I was going to die.

My workdays were intense and then coming home to more work on the van and my YouTube channel was just too much at times. After a few months on the road, all those feelings of panic and anxiety just disappeared. One day I realized, I haven't had a panic attack in a while. Another day I realized, this situation should stress me out, but it doesn't. After I got over that initial hump, van life has really been the cure for the stressed-out New Yorker that was living inside of me.

This way of life is not for everyone. Maybe you'll never get over those fears and anxieties. Maybe you'll get into the van and a few months later realize you'd rather be at home. I'm not saying this lifestyle is a cure all, it was just a cure for me. I wanted to include this chapter so you know you're not alone if you don't feel amazing on day one. As with any big change, there is going to be an adjustment period. Whether that's a day, week, or month, listen to your body, feel the feelings, and allow life on the road to become your new panacea.

Minimalist Lifestyle

One of the biggest surprises when entering into van life is how minimalist you can be. I've spent my whole life buying things, the latest fashions, cool new gadgets, home decor and the like. I used to love wandering through the mall and coming home with bags full of treasure.

Even grocery shopping was a treat because with endless space in my home-sized fridge and pantry, I could buy whatever tickled my fancy with no regard for where I was going to stash it when I got home. When you live in a van, there just isn't room for anything nonessential.

Nowadays, I don't buy anything unless we absolutely need it. And even then, we have a discussion to flush out if that need *really* is a need or if it's a *want*. Our home only has so much storage and that space is already pretty full.

I don't have room for new clothes unless I get rid of old clothes. I don't have a cupboard for a new kitchen gadget unless I get rid of dry goods that let us stay off grid for longer.
Plus, so many of the pretty trinkets you can buy on the road are breakable and a bouncy van is no place for anything that will smash into a million pieces when it hits the floor.

When we moved out of our apartment and into the van, I was shocked at how much stuff we were living with. Clothes, sports equipment and kitchen tools that were never used. We donated bag after bag of stuff to local charities and sold thousands of dollars' worth of things we thought we needed at some point in time.

I read once that all the junk you're living with used to be money. As I was hauling garbage bags full of stuff out of our home, I had the revelation that I would be a lot richer were it not for all these things.

We met a lovely woman on the road who was traveling in a beautiful RV style, manufacturer built, campervan that cost well over $100,000. When she rolled up to our riverside campsite and asked if she could park up with us for the night, we were in awe of her luxury rig. After chatting and getting to know each other better she offered to let us see inside her tiny home on wheels.

When she opened the slider door, I kid you not, garbage rolled out of her van and on to the floor. Stepping inside I had to navigate where to put my feet since there was stuff everywhere. Tons of books, clothes and knickknacks on every single surface including the floor.

Her luxury home felt claustrophobic because of all the stuff she was trying to jam in it. It was like she took every single thing from her home, skipped the downsizing process, and shoved it all into her van. I do not recommend living like that.

Life on the road is simple, you need very few things to be happy. A couple of different outfits suitable for varying weather (you end up wearing the same things day in day out anyways). A few tools to cook and eat your meals with. Some actual tools to work on your van. Add in a few toys to enhance outdoor activities and maybe some camera gear to capture it with - that's about it.

We've been taught all our lives that: we need more; buy more; accumulate more; and the more you have the more successful you are. But when you enter van life, you'll discover what you really need is less.

By having less, you get to experience more. You get to travel more places and see more wonderful things. By letting go of societal norms you open your mind and your life to endless possibilities that might make you a better human - watch out!

It's amazing to see your life transform in so many ways because of van life. Becoming a minimalist, whether you want to self-identify that way or not, is just one of those many transitions that might take some getting used to.

It will feel so freeing when you finally let go of the stuff holding you back and embrace the simplicity of life.

Daily Costs on The Road

Just like the budget we discussed previously; your daily costs will vary based on your preferences. The more you eat out or visit paid camping locations, the more expensive your life will be.

We chose to stealth camp and cook for ourselves as much as possible to stretch our dollars and days on the road to the max. Yes, we splurge from time to time and enjoy the nice things in life - mainly tacos. We saved a good amount of money to be able to enjoy van life, we didn't want to say no to new experiences because they cost too much.

One big change we had to get used to was the mentality of spending versus saving. We spent an entire year saving as much money as we could and budgeting as best we could to keep costs down on our build.

Then we got on the road and had a tough time feeling good about spending the money we had saved. It was weird to let go of that frugal mentality, to enjoy the fruits of our labors. As people who were used to getting that weekly paycheck, it felt scary not to have anything reliable coming in.

What we've learned is that it's important to give and receive freely when it comes to money. Don't hold on to it so tightly that it becomes painful to spend and don't block the flow towards you by saying no to opportunities or turning down a kind gesture (we got three tomatoes in one day from 2 strangers – I'd call that a win!).

Not that we're going around blowing our money. We're still very deliberate about the choices we make and the experiences we enjoy. As I've said, we like to buy groceries and cook most of our meals at home.

But from time to time, there's nothing better than enjoying a local delicacy or going out for dinner at the best reviewed restaurant in town. Oddly enough, most of the time we go out to eat we end up meeting really cool people.

We generally sit at the bar (even if we're not drinking) and strike up conversations with the bartender and patrons. We've also made some really good friends just from saying hello in random coffee shops. If you completely isolate yourself inside your van, you'll miss out on all these wonderful interactions.

We spend on average $200 a month on groceries and $200 a month at restaurants and coffee shops. Since COVID of course this is a bit more complicated as people can't sit around bars and don't mingle at coffee shops, *oh the days....* Now we make most of our new van life friends at boondocking locations or grocery store parking lots.

One of the biggest costs on the road is fuel. Whether that's gas or diesel, eventually you're going to have to fill your tank. The less mobile you are, the less money you have to budget for gas. If your plan is to get somewhere and spend a full month at the same camp spot with minimal trips and grocery store runs, you can spend almost nothing. But if you're doing a lot of driving, it's going to cost you.

We spent a ton on gas our first few months of travel. We started out trying to snowboard 71 mountains in a single season which was a whole lot of miles costing a whole lot of money. We were moving so fast we spent an average of $500 a month on diesel.

Keep in mind, diesel prices go up in the winter because it's also a heating fuel. So higher winter prices plus tons of driving meant that one month we spent $900! Now that we've slowed down a lot, we're averaging about $200 a month.

GasBuddy is an app that shows you all the prices for gas around you. You can set it to show pricing for the fuel type you need and then pull up either a list or a map of everything nearby. I'll often pull up the map and see that the closest gas stations are awfully expensive and if we just drive an additional 30 miles down the road, we can save big.

I would be so annoyed if we filled up at $3.02/gallon and 30 miles later saw it was only $2.70/gallon. If you get the GasBuddy debit card, you can activate bonus deals for up to $0.25 off a gallon.

The app is crowd sourced so you can also submit gas prices to earn points that can win you free gas. We've saved hundreds of dollars between lower gas prices and the extra savings offered by the card. I highly recommend GasBuddy. (Use code EH2BR6N to register). Still waiting to win the free gas gift cards they give away every day.

We spend a lot more time in coffee shops than I ever imagined we would. Coffee shops are a big part of our internet solution so we're often going inside to get Wi-Fi for a few hours and then feel obligated to buy something. I feel like it would be quite rude to just use the Wi-Fi and not become a patron.

We try to find local places that have big comfy chairs and cool art over corporate conglomerates but it's not always possible – I do feel slightly less bad just using the Wi-Fi at a big corporation.

In any case we're spending on average $50 or more a month on coffee shops. Another 2020 update, after the pandemic, it's a bit tricker to find shops where you can sit and chill, but they are coming back slowly and someday we will be back to normal I'm sure of it.

Our final great big variable expense is vehicle maintenance. Because we had an older van with a lot of miles on her, Frankie was constantly tinkering with the engine.

We've had to replace parts, pay mechanics to fix her up and buy way more oil than we should have because we had an oil leak (since repaired!). This was one of the big reasons we decided to sell our first rig, a 2003 and upgrade to a newer van, a 2019.

We were tired of spending money and time every month fixing this or that or tinkering to try and make her better. There was nothing majorly wrong with Lolo but an older vehicle will come with more maintenance, that's just a given.

It is worth thinking about the maintenance on newer vehicles too. A friend of ours has a 2020 Mercedes Revel. The 10,000 mile tune up at Mercedes cost over $1,000. Just like a home, a van needs some money put into it from time to time to make sure she's tip top so be sure to set aside a slush fund for that.

Along with all these variable expenses, you will also have fixed expenses. We paid for our insurance (vehicle and renters) up front for the whole year so we wouldn't have to think about it for 12 months ($1,900). If you can get your van insured as an RV this will be much less expensive.

Some states and some providers won't allow this but shop around till you find one that will. We have the renter's policy on top of the vehicle policy to cover our personal belongings like laptops and cameras. If we got broken into or wrecked, our vehicle policy covers up to $15,000 in custom modifications on the van (our build) and the renters policy covers the stuff we are traveling with.

Our gym membership was $22 per month combined (Planet Fitness) until we had to upgrade gyms post COVID-19 for a smaller and more shower friendly option at $80 per month (Anytime Fitness).

We are considering if not having a gym membership at all would be feasible since we've been loving truck stop showers so much lately. For less than $15 you can have an unlimited hot water shower in a locked room with a sink, toilet, and shower. It's luxurious for us vanlifers. My only concern is that we might not be able to find truck stop showers in bigger cities.

Health insurance was $178 each per month for a cost sharing program (Christian Health Care Ministries) but our nomadic friends told us about World Nomads and now it's only $150 per month for both of us. For us, this is in case of emergency only (oh, shit!) health coverage. We don't have any existing medical conditions and do not require monthly prescriptions.

If you are someone who needs a more comprehensive plan, you might be shocked at the price of even an extremely high deductible plan. If you're from outside the US and have socialized health care, you might only want to look at traveler's insurance for when you're outside your home country. However, if you're American, you'll need something more robust. Break a leg and you might limp out of the hospital with an astronomical bill.

Our two cell phones used to cost $120 total on T-Mobile, but the service was so spotty we had to switch to Verizon at $160 per month. Since we now depend on our cell phones and internet to make a living, we couldn't afford to be off grid so often, and after discussing with many other nomads, it was clear Verizon service was the best.

Finally, for subscriptions, we have $10 per month photo editing software, both my sister and Frankie's sister let us mooch off their Netflix (thanks!) and that's it.

We got rid of any other costs that we're going to be a drain on us financially, even a few dollars a month makes a difference. Everyone's van life budget will be different and depend completely on their circumstances, necessities and wants. What matters is that you know what you're spending and how much you have so you never live beyond your means.

Travel Companions

You've probably already got a good idea of who your travel companions are. If you and your partner are planning together, just going out on a limb here, you're probably going to travel together. If you've got two kids, you're not going to leave them behind (although to some that might sound appealing at times). For those of you looking to go it alone or with a pet, know that it's totally doable too. Van life families come in all shapes and sizes - there is no right answer here.

There are, however, both joys and complications that come with every travel companion arrangement. For solo travelers, you may feel the need to beef up security or find a convoy of likeminded travelers. It's also possible you'll experience more loneliness and you have no one to share the burden of maintenance, van choices and expenses.

Many people choose solo van life because their goal is to break out on their own and see the world on their terms, develop self-confidence or escape a bad situation. They need time and space to examine their thoughts, to empower their souls. Others simply don't have anyone in their lives interested in traveling with them and they are tired of waiting. Whatever the reason, solo travelers are admirable and I wish I had the gumption when I was in my early 20s. My journal would be full of amazing adventures to look back on fondly.

Couples get to share costs and workload but also put their relationship's feet to the fire. The stress and challenges that come with living on the road are like a pressure cooker for bad relationships. If you don't have great communication or conflict resolution skills, you might end up becoming a solo traveler. The benefit to traveling with a partner is that you get to see and share the joy and adventure of the journey with them.

You have someone to sit around the campfire with, to push you out of your comfort zone, to laugh and cry with. That's if you can stand each other for long enough to get to experience all these joys (although, if you survived quarantine together, you can definitely do van life).

I've heard many tales of woe from couples that breakup after living on the road together for a few months or partners who backed out weeks before the journey was set to begin. But also, many success stories of couples who have thrived, whose relationship is stronger than ever and who absolutely love having their partner to share this adventure with (I don't want to jinx anything here but Frankie and I are in the "doing great" category).

Before we got into this Frankie and I laid out the financial implications for our investment if we split. He would buy the van outright up front and that would be his. I would split the cost of the build and expenses on the road. If we did breakup, I could walk away and feel good knowing I didn't lose all my money.

I would consider my initial investment my rent for all the time we shared on the road. If you are traveling as a duo and both investing in the van, you really need to have these talks before you open your checkbook. Of course, if you're married everything is 50/50 anyways but if not, make sure you both agree to the money arrangements. This goes for friends buying a van together too. The biggest thing couples fight about is money. Get this squared away so you don't have to worry about it.

Family life on the road also comes with so many joys. You get to watch your kids explore and play and see new worlds. The memories you make will last a lifetime even if they are tales of ineptitude or hilarious hijinks. Your kids learn to appreciate the great outdoors and become students of mother nature, they become self-sufficient and street smart.

There's also the reality that life with kids has its own very real and exhausting challenges: nap times; hangry tantrums; hissy fits; home schooling; and sleeping arrangements. You're pretty much guaranteeing that you and your partner will never have alone time which can put a strain on your relationship too.

Safety concerns for traveling with children include the fact that each human needs a chair and street legal seatbelt. A temperature-controlled space is a must if they are old enough to be left alone in the van (same goes for pets). You'll also have to get creative in finding ways for everyone to sleep comfortably.

I do think this is a great way to raise kids that exposes them to a world beyond their small neighborhood, to various cultures, different ways of life, people who look nothing like themselves and heaps of adventure. I hope that someday I can share my experiences with a baby on the road and then I'll really know what it's like.

I could be way off base here because you never really know what it's like to be a parent, until you're a parent. I'll probably have to write another book just about the realities of it whenever we get to that stage of life.

Van life with a pet also has some considerations. First, what kind of pet are we talking here? Are you going to have a cat, dog, snake, ant farm, fish? The possibilities are endless. If you need a glass cage for your pet, make sure this it's very secure along with everything in it. You don't want rocks flying around inside the glass case when you stop suddenly.

The most common pets on the road are dogs and cats. Firstly, you're going to have to see if your pet even likes being on the road and spending large amounts of time in a moving vehicle. Some animals just don't like being in vehicles no matter how comfy you try and make it for them.

Next you should really have your dog or cat buckled up while driving because they will become a projectile if you get into an accident. Then you have to think about waste, fur everywhere, drool, water and food, all of which will cause you to have to clean your space more often. Of course, since you love your pet none of that will matter.

The reason we decided not to get a dog at first, even though we really wanted to, was that we were planning on doing a lot of border crossings. At each check point, extra paperwork would have been required showing vaccines and ownership. There's also the possibility that your pet will get sick or hurt along the way and need veterinary care. For us this were all complications we didn't need especially as the van build process was such a stress that we had no time to welcome a pet into our family.

When COVID hit and our dreams of driving all the way to Panama were put on indefinite hold, we decided it was time to find our puppy. After about a month of searching we found Paco at a Humane Society in Brookings, Oregon. Initially we were worried that the adoption agency would have an issue with our living situation.

Many of the pet profiles we saw online required a fully fenced in yard which we obviously wouldn't be able to provide. Another van life friend of ours said she fibbed a little at her adoption appointment, saying that her home base was in California and she was on a road trip, which was kind of true but she had no intention of going back to that home base anytime soon.

When we went to meet Paco, we were upfront and honest about the fact we live and travel in a van. The woman running the agency was immediately thrilled. She had adopted to people who travel in RVs before and rightly stated this is the best way for dogs to live. She knew Paco would be a great hiking dog (which he is) and that he would be awesome on the road (also true).

Life with Paco did require a bit of adjustment, we can't go on certain hikes with him and we have to keep his needs at the forefront of our day. Overall, it's been amazing getting to know, love, and welcome Paco into our lives. Watching his joy for life is infectious - from exploring new landscapes, sleeping on Frankie's shoulders, snuggling up to us on the couch and his unbridled enthusiasm at the smallest things.

No matter who you choose to travel with, your level of communication will dictate your results. There is no room in a tiny home for passive aggressive jabs or great big fights, no space for bad feelings to fester. Frankie and I have often had to turn to one another and say "that thing you said really upset me" or "I'm feeling really frustrated that…". Somehow this doesn't turn into a fight but rather a discussion about what happened and how we can do better.

I am as amazed at this as you are. The fact of the matter is, you don't have a spare room to storm off too, or really any private space at all (except maybe the woods). Although it's still important to have alone time and activities you enjoy solo, the majority of your time will be spent with each other. You've got to have a strong relationship for it to survive this alternative lifestyle.

Travel companions can make the dumpiest locations into the best nights of your life. On the flip side, a bad travel companion can turn the most scenic vista into a nightmare. We've all been on trips with someone who was a drag making the adventure more of a chore than an enjoyable getaway. You do not want to enter into van life with someone like that - trust me. Choose your van life companion with extreme care.

Where to Go to The Bathroom

This is by far the number one (or number two... get it?!) question we get asked about van life. It seems everyone is worried about where they will do their business if they don't have a house. But let me ask you this – have you ever been on a road trip, spent a whole day hiking in the woods or shopping at a mall? Have you ever, in your whole life, done your business somewhere other than in the comfort of your own home?

As someone who's had gastrointestinal issues my whole life, I certainly have. For me, it's always been important to know where the closest bathroom is. When moving into the van, having a toilet on board was 100% a necessity for me.

For our first build we went with a super basic composting toilet that was literally a bucket with a seat on it. We also had a urine diverter that shot right out the bottom of the truck directly to the ground. The biggest issue with this wasn't number two but number one.

You couldn't (or shouldn't) use the pee option in the city on pavement when there's a toilet available, it makes for a big stinky mess. But it's perfect for the middle of nowhere camping situations when you would be peeing outside anyways. Dirt acts as a great filter.

The urine diverter is a must especially in the middle of the night when you wake up in your pajamas and need to go. The idea of getting out of the van in the pitch-black to find somewhere to go is not appealing, especially in the middle of winter. Being able to go inside your nice warm van then jump right back into bed is amazing.

Plus, there's little to no clean up involved. After you go, use a spray bottle with a mix of water, white vinegar (or a more powerful biodegradable cleaner) and spritz the diverter down. Then toss any toilet paper in the trash and you're done. This option is about as cheap as peeing in a jug but comes with less user error accidents, aka you can't tip it over while using it and end up with pee everywhere.

For our second build we're going with the same theory but a more professional version. This bucket toilet from Etsy is a perfect low-cost solution that we are going to modify to have a second spout activated with a switch that goes right out the bottom of the truck like Lolo had because pee buckets fill up fast and stink real bad.

The number two area requires a bit more cleanup but is by far the cheapest way to have a legit emergency place to number 2 in your van. You can line the whole bucket with a garbage bag (or not) and then add a composting material, just enough to cover the bottom (we use peat moss and dirt from the local hardware store).

After you go, add a layer of composting material, close the lid and you're done. Once it gets full, you can dig a hole in the woods and burry the materials (without a garbage bag) or you can tie up the garbage bag and throw it in a dumpster. This really works well and surprisingly doesn't smell. Unlike the next option.

Next, you can get really cheap and use plastic bottles for pee and shopping bags for poop. We've only had to pee in a jug once or twice but there's a joke in the van life community that you never want to rob a vanlifer because we've all got a bottle of pee somewhere that we could throw on you – yuck.

The number 2 in a bag has unfortunately been the only option a few times. Before we were comfortable with the composting toilet, we had 1 or two emergencies that we didn't want to use the bucket for.

These emergencies came when there were no public bathrooms around and we weren't far enough into the woods to dig a hole. The bag of poop works great actually but as you can imagine there is a smell that goes with it. You're going to want to get rid of that bag responsibly ASAP, even if it's triple bagged the stink still comes through, seriously.

The next most common toilet set ups are manufactured composting toilets. These separate urine from poop. The urine compartment is basically a big jug that fills up quickly. If you didn't know, urine smells something fierce when it's left to chill for a while.

So, this bucket needs to be emptied almost daily depending on how often you're using it. The poop section works like the composting bucket I described above but it has a fancy crank that turns the composting material which helps it break down and an airtight lid.

Most people go with the NaturesHead toilet, but we've heard the AirHead toilet is smaller and works better. NaturesHead composting compartment needs to be emptied every three weeks or so whereas AirHead can go up to three months. These toilets come about a $1,000 price tag, just slightly more expensive than a bucket.

Most RVs have black water tanks which allow the toilet inside to act like a regular house toilet. While this seems lovely at first (you get to flush!), you're going to have to dump that black water eventually and unlike grey water that you can generally get away with dumping in the woods, black water must be disposed of responsibly at official black water dump locations.

You'll find these at almost all campgrounds, RV parks and sometimes at National Parks or other places RVs frequent like gas stations. You can set your iOverlander app to tell you where these receptacles are and I've heard they are actually very easy to find once you start looking. In my mind, the convenience of having a real toilet, doesn't outweigh the stinky job of dumping the black water tank. It's just one more chore I don't want to have to deal with.

The final option is kind of like an RV toilet with the black water tank attached to it. It's called a cassette toilet and you use a chemical mix to keep the smell at bay. It usually has a few gallon tank and when it needs to be dumped, rather than needing a legit black water dump site, all you need is a toilet.

You remove the black water canister and flush away the remnants. These are way cheaper than fancy composting toilets and less annoying to dump than RV toilets. Sounds great right? Well sure, if you don't mind the smell. Even with the chemical concoctions you have to add to keep the smells at bay, it somehow always smells like a dirty urinal infusing your van with an *eau du poop*.

There are a few more options, like dry flush (you have to keep buying their bags) or incinerator (fannnnncy but needs electricity just like the dry flush). But no matter which toilet option you go with, you're going to want to do your business outside of the van as much as possible.

The less you go in the van, the less frequently you have to empty your toilet, pee jug or black water tank. Like most chores, the less often you have to do them, the better. The best way to prolong the amount of time between dumps (pun intended) is to go in public washrooms or dig nice sized holes in the woods.

You might feel awkward at first entering a place of business just to use the bathroom but after a while you won't even think twice about walking in proudly to do your business and walking right out. Have we all forgotten about the classic storybook *Everyone Poops*? It's true! That's why there are public bathrooms literally everywhere.

Whether you live in a van or not, you never know when your lunch is going to do a back flip in your stomach and need to be mass evacuated.

To prove to you that you can really go anywhere and that there's no need to be worried about this simple human act at all, here is a ridiculously long list of places with public washrooms:
- Restaurants
- Fast food chains
- Roadside diners
- Gas stations
- Hotel lobbies
- Rest stations along the highway
- Grocery stores
- Big box stores
- Any tourist traps
- Hardware stores
- Coffee shops
- Book stores
- Family or friends' houses
- Libraries
- Doctors' offices
- Community centers
- Flea markets
- Farmers markets
- Gyms (even if you're not a member you can ask the front desk)
- Tanning salons
- Campgrounds
- RV parks
- Laundry mats
- Public pools

- Public parks
- Random porta potties
- The great outdoors

If you're far away from civilization, it doesn't matter where you go. If you don't have a toilet on board, grab a shovel and cop a squat at the side of the road. Crouched down in a deep squat is actually the healthiest position to poop from. You can even bring a carry sized shovel on your hikes. Now you know, you're welcome. Just make sure to bury everything nicely so no one accidently steps in it and the toilet paper doesn't float away in the wind.

If you're really close to civilization, you'll have no problem finding one of the facilities I've listed above. If it's a big public place, there's no need to buy anything to use the bathroom. But if it's a smaller mom and pop operation, the respectable thing to do would be to buy at least something from the shop.

Here's the caveat. It's important to be careful about what you eat while you're on the road. I know for certain that dairy runs out of my body faster than a world class sprinter at the Olympics. Knowing this about my digestive track, I'm not going to down an ice cream cone or mac and cheese, even though they are oh so tasty, unless I know I'm going to be near a reliable toilet later.

For example, we were staying outside a friend's house and I had a craving for ice cream. I went for it. Got a double scoop, cookie dough and pralines and cream. I fully enjoyed that cone and didn't regret it at all. Until it woke me up in the middle of the night and needed it out of my body *immediately.*

No problem, I just went into my friend's house and did my business. I would never in a million years make that ice cream choice if we were going to be doing an 8-hour drive with an unknown sleeping location.

Where we go to the bathroom is one of the most asked questions, but it need not be. There are so many simple solutions on board and out in the real world for you to take care of your business. Many van builds don't have any set up for washroom facilities at all. We're happy to have a pretty basic set up. Others need the full shebang.

It's a personal choice that will likely be driven by budget. We didn't want to spend $1,000 on a toilet so we made a low-cost choice. We're happy with the setup we have but if someone wanted to send us a fancy toilet, we'd probably say yes.

A COVID update for you. It has become a bit more difficult to find public washrooms since the pandemic. Some are now closed to the public and some shops are now drive through only so you don't have the ability to go in and use their facility. This was worse at the very beginning but now that most places are entering various phases of reopening there are more options, but certainly not as many as pre-pandemic.

You can still count on places like grocery and big box stores, but smaller establishments might not want the hassle. The flipside of this is that since the pandemic we're spending more time out in the middle of nowhere so we can go in the woods no problem.

"I wandered everywhere, through cities and countries wide. And everywhere I went, the world was on my side." — Roman Payne

Where to Sleep

Another anxiety of mine before starting out on this journey was where we were going to park our van to sleep. You hear about the dreaded horror stories on the internet of vanlifers getting *the knock* in the middle of the night and being told to leave.

The first few nights we stealth camped I was a ball of nerves. In my mind, there was nothing more mortifying than the prospect of having to get out of bed in the middle of the night to find somewhere else to go. Frankie on the other hand thought nothing of it "If they ask us to leave, we leave. That's it". And realistically, that is it. You get the dreaded knock; you move on and you're all good except for some lost sleep.

Where you can sleep will depend a lot on your rig. Most vanlifers have white work truck style vans or other similar vehicles that from the outside look like any other van. These rigs have the dual benefit of being able to get down some gnarly dirt roads and blend into any city street.

Others have great big rigs, RVs, camper trailers, truck bed popups and the like all of which are obviously homes on wheels, may not be able to go down too many forestry roads and would stick out in a city. Lolo was very stealthy (maybe less so with her giant mural) and could blend into a parking lot or residential/city street easily. Most rigs can park most places but some might require special RV lots depending on the area you're traveling though.

Some towns are super van friendly, others, not so much. In many places, the number of people who have to live in their cars because they can't afford rent is at an all-time high. I'm sure due to the pandemic this number is just going to rise. Many municipalities see this as a disturbance.

How dare someone park their home in my neighborhood, I pay property taxes and the city should get rid of these free loaders. To me, this seems incredibly heartless. As a van dweller myself, I hope that I'm always welcome on your block as long as I respect it and follow the rules outlined below. But it's never a bad idea to do a quick internet search and see what the bylaws are in the area you're looking to camp.

On the flip side, I'm sure there are a few bad apples making a bad name for the rest of us. People who park in the same location for weeks at a time; are loud or inconsiderate to their surroundings; people who leave trash wherever they go; or who flagrantly live out of their vans by say, starting up their BBQ on the sidewalk.

If, however, you follow these few simple rules, you shouldn't have any issues parking overnight in any legal location.

1. ***Don't Overstay Your Welcome*** – we tend to move around and stay at different locations almost every night. Of course, if you're out in the wilderness and find a great boondocking spot, you can usually stay for up to two weeks. If you're staying on a friend's property or you have express permission to remain in the same location, you can stay as long as you're invited to. For the more public and city style options like parking lots, you're going to start to draw attention to yourself if you're there longer than a day or two, especially if you're not vacating during the day.

2. ***Don't Make a Mess*** – The old campers adage applies here: take nothing but memories, leave nothing but footprints. Your tiny home on wheels should be a self-contained unit. No garbage flying out the windows, no fluids leaking out the back. Respect your surroundings and leave them the way you found them, if not better.

3. **Read the Signs** – If a sign says you can't park there, don't park there. We once rolled up to a neighborhood off the highway that had giant signs posted all around that there was no street parking from 1am to 5am. So, we left and found somewhere else to park (a hotel parking lot if you're curious). If you're not breaking the law and respecting the no parking signs, you've got a significantly lower chance of getting woken up in the middle of the night.
4. **Go Stealth Mode** – When we pull up for the night in a more urban setting, we immediately get Lolo ready for bed. Engine off, blackout window covers on, lights down low. I thought the list would be longer but that's really it. From the outside it looks like our van is empty, inside we're cooking dinner or getting ready for bed. Just like when you get home to a house and start your evening routine, we do the same thing. We just do it inside our van in a random location.
5. **Arrive Late, Leave Early** – Timing is everything. If you're parking in a city or neighborhood in front of someone's house, arriving after they are tucked away for the night is a great way to avoid being noticed. Leaving in a timely manner also takes away the ability of nosy neighbors to wonder who you are for too long.
6. **Look for Clues** – Are there other camper style vehicles in the same lot? Where have they chosen to park? If it looks like they know what they're

doing, follow their lead. If they look like they're breaking a bunch of these rules, move along.
7. ***Ask Around*** – If you're really not sure, ask. We've asked security guards, gas station attendants, and locals to name a few. All have been very helpful and guided us to our best night's sleep or assured us that no one would bother us where we were at. You could even ask the local police department if you want to be extra careful.
8. ***Back In*** – Last but not least this might be the most crucial tip. Always park your rig so that you can boogie out of there in a moment's notice. If you have to grab your keys, start the car and go, it's a heck of a lot easier to drive straight forward than having to back out of the spot make a K turn and then go.

Although lots of places are cracking down on sleeping in your vehicle (mainly big cities experiencing issues with homeless populations living in their vehicles and now because of COVID and I'm sure a few bad eggs, even Walmart's aren't as friendly), there are still a number of tried-and-true locations to call home for a night.

Here's a compilation of locations that you could easily shack up for a night for free:
- 24-hour gyms
- 24-hour grocery stores (and even some non-24-hour grocery stores)
- Casinos
- Hospitals
- Walmart (check the location as they are all independently managed)
- Cracker Barrel
- Hotels
- BLM (Bureau of Land Management land, mostly on the West Coast of the US)
- Forestry land
- The middle of nowhere at the top of a mountain
- Busy residential neighborhoods with lots of cars already parked on the street
- City streets with no "no parking" signs or other parking restrictions
- Some ski resorts
- Highway rest areas
- Marinas
- Parks

It's certainly more relaxing to find a place to park for the night when the city in question is welcoming to vanlifers. We've been in towns where it seems like we are social pariahs, no overnight parking signs everywhere and warnings on Facebook groups that *this place*, it doesn't like our kind.

Speaking of Facebook groups, these can be very helpful when trying to find a safe place to park overnight. Look for groups about van life or RV dwellers and you'll find a plethora of information about all things related to this lifestyle. Last winter we found a group specific to vanlifers who ski and snowboard with information about where to park at each ski resort, so handy.

One of the most helpful aspects of these groups is that you can find city specific information about where to park for the night. You can also ask for help if your search within the group wasn't fruitful. Facebook groups are great for help and advice for all aspects of van life including where to sleep.

I highly recommend you join a few with the fair warning that along with the help, there's a lot of junk too (and some incredibly angry judgmental people, but that's a story for another chapter).

In addition to these groups, there are several apps and websites that highlight safe places to park in which the nomad community helps each other out by adding or editing location details. iOverlander is a must – this is the biggest and most popular and has the most listings.

These apps will help you find free accommodations, paid camp sites, locations for water fill ups, black water dumping, and so much more. There are also many websites that offer free accommodation, but some require you to be a member with a low annual fee. As you travel be sure to update listings with additional information and add your own finds to help the community.

There are also of course paid places to park where you can be 100% certain you are able to stay the night. These are almost always listed in the free apps (I generally have my filter set not to even show them because I know I'm not paying to stay there).

As the van life community is exploding, more aps and websites are popping up to allow homeowners to make their property available for campgrounds and tiny home on wheels travelers (think Airbnb for vanlifers).

Here are a few of the tried-and-true options:
- iOverlander app
- www.FreeCampsites.net

- www.Hipcamp.com
- www.BoondockersWelcome.com
- www.HarvestHost.com
- AllStays app

After those first few anxious nights sleeping in the van, I find sleeping on the road incredibly comfortable. We've got a cozy home to relax in every single night wherever we are.

Often, I'll forget that we're in a random parking lot at the side of the highway or wherever we might be because, I'm in my home. When you're in a brick-and-mortar house, you don't think about the neighborhood, you just enjoy your space.

The same is true of a van. That's what's wonderful about van life, it's extended travel with all the comforts of home and, in my opinion, it's perfection.

But of course, the best night's sleep is to be found deep in nature, far away from the traffic and noise of the city or highway. Where the stars shine brighter than you've ever seen and the only noise is an owl hooting in the distance.

We see so many vanlifers choose the Walmart and Cracker Barrel options over and over again and I just don't get the appeal. Sure, they are great for a one-night easy pass through when you're tired from driving, but as a regular choice, they are not my cup of tea.

The first time we slept at Walmart (about 4 months into our travels), we woke up with a flat tire. That was a good enough omen for us not to go back for a very long time. Although, having a tire center right there was very handy. The second time we stayed at a Walmart we were actually kind of stuck waiting for a package to be delivered to the local UPS Store.

With that delay plus the insane temperature drop, it got down to 14 degrees F (-10 degrees C), and the fact the town we were in didn't have any other boondocking options, we figured we may as well stay close to somewhere with all the supplies we could ever need.

Where to sleep at night might worry you at first but once you're on the road you'll see it's really not that big of a deal. As with all things van life, you'll get into a rhythm and routine around your sleeping preferences.

Nowadays we don't even think or worry about where we're going to sleep until well into the day when we realize the sun will be setting soon. There are so many options when you start looking, and even if the nearest option is 30 minutes away, you're in a vehicle so it's not hard to get there!

Where to Shower

Just like going to the bathroom, taking a shower is something we all do. I should say, it's something I sincerely hope we all do, the less stinky people the better. Housers (people who don't live van life) have this image of vanlifers that we are dirty or smell bad but that's really not the case (okay sometimes it might be, but when we need to clean up, we absolutely do).

There are people who work full time jobs while living in their vans and no one is the wiser. They show up to work every single day, hair combed, face shaved, smelling like a million bucks. You'd have no idea they lived in a van by looking at them.

It's slightly more complicated to find a shower than it is to find a bathroom but it's still totally doable. Lots of builds have showers built in, indoor, outdoor or both. While this is a nice luxury it's not a necessity. Here's a list of places, some paid for, some public, some natural, where you can soap up.

You can also always set the filter on iOverlander to show you all the shower locations in your area:
- Gyms

- Public pools
- Recreation centers
- Spas
- Hot springs
- Campgrounds
- Public beaches
- Natural water sources (lakes/rivers/etc.)

Just be sure to have biodegradable soap on hand if you are choosing to shower in nature or will be dumping your grey tank on the road. If you absolutely must have a shower on board there are a few options. The first is of course a traditional shower. You can build a fully waterproof "closet" with running water.

Have it hooked up to a hot water heater, draining to a grey water tank and you're good to go. This is of course the most expensive option. Building and plumbing a waterproof box is more complicated than it sounds.

There are tons of shower build options on YouTube including recirculating systems that have their own tank and filtration system so that you'll never run out of water.

You'll also want to make sure you get a very low-flow showerhead with an on off button so that you're not blowing through water. Typical house showers use gallons per minute If you only have 20-30 gallons on board, you might only have enough water for a few minutes of showering if you're thinking conservation first.

The other consideration with a stationary shower is the space you need to allocate for it in your build. When you have less than 200 square feet, every square inch matters. For our first and now second builds, we didn't want to have the traditional floor to ceiling shower because it chops the space in half visually and, in my opinion, makes the space feel smaller.

This is another reason why we have so few upper cabinets. We want to keep our build light, airy and open. However, I've seen tons of builds that achieve that look and also have a shower so it's not totally going to destroy the appearance of your build if you choose to install one - don't worry.

If you're going to give up that much space, it has to serve a dual purpose. Most people add a composting toilet to their showers as it makes sense for your bathroom to be contained in one space, plus it has a door for added privacy.

It also often becomes a storage space when you're not showering for items like a laundry bin, skis, wet gear (because it's a great place let things hang to dry) and of course towels. Think about it, even if you shower every day, that's only about 5-10 minutes of the whole day the shower is in use. It's completely useless the rest of the time, unless you give it a dual purpose.

Next up is the wet dream of those with engineering minds, the hidden shower. I've seen lots of people attempt this and only a few get it right. Cabinets that pop open to reveal a tiled drainage hole and pop-up shower curtains. Old RVs were hilariously bad at this with sliding floors and hoops for curtains. When we were van shopping, we toured an old RV with a flat cabinet that opened up to reveal a shower. I took one look at the shower and knew the disgusting carpet floor had been soaking wet many times.

Our particular solution to the hidden shower is the drawer shower. A simple laundry sink is pulled out from under the couch. It's got a drainage pipe that goes right out to the earth (not unlike what would happen if you showered outside). The curtain rod fits inside the sink and when you're ready to shower you lift it up and hook it into the ceiling. Our water comes from the kitchen sink. We have an attachable shower head that reaches to the "shower" and also out the side door for outdoor use.

I've also seen a very fancy version of this where the shower basin is hidden in the toe kick area and drains through the main floor which has been tiled and sealed to flow directly to the earth.

These options are great, especially in a post COVID world since it's more important than ever to have some way to shower onboard. Sure, baby wipes work for a time but eventually you're going to want a full shower.

Because of the size constraints and water limitations, is your shower going to be somewhere you want to lounge after a long day? Sadly not. Does it get you clean and make you feel fresh as a daisy, yes. Sometimes that's all that matters.

Having an outdoor shower set up is great but of course this only works in warmer climates and more remote places.

I don't think you're going to want to take an outdoor shower in the middle of winter in downtown Manhattan – I could be wrong, you do you. But the ability to hose off yourself, or your dirty gear (or dog!) outside the van is very handy. I mentioned above that our simple system works off the kitchen sink to allow us to shower inside and outside.

Many vans are set up with an additional shower port out the back doors of their vans which this gives the option to rig up a shower curtain between your back doors so you can shower privately. You can also purchase portable hot water showers that use buckets full of lake water and are actually a really nice option.

The most primitive shower option is the shower bag. These are sturdy rubber bags that, when left in the sun all day, provide a warm shower. You hang the bag so gravity can work the water through the attached shower head to your body.

These do work, but can take forever to heat up and if it's not warm enough, they won't heat up at all so you either have a cool shower or you can boil and add hot water. They also provide little to no water pressure so getting the suds out of your thick hair might be tricky.

Next up is the portable propane shower I mention above - now this is luxury. Grab a bucket of river or lake water, start the propane heater and be amazed when the shower head releases a powerful blast of hot water. Definitely the way to go if you want a luxurious outdoor shower with no worries about water consumption.

You will need to stock up on little green propane tanks though or purchase low pressure regulators and other fittings to have the water heater connected to a bigger propane tank. When we were first thinking about our build layout, we very much wanted a shower on board.

At home we took showers almost daily and sometimes Frankie would shower twice a day, before and after work. Because we were so used to the unlimited hot water and showers whenever we wanted, we imagined we would be very stinky without it. It only took a few weeks on the road to realize, although it's relaxing and oh so nice to have a shower every day, you really don't need one.

Sure after a few days you start to notice a bit of a funk, but any true vanlifer would be happy to clean up with a wet wipe if needed. Sometimes you just need to wash your pits and ditch (armpits and private parts) to feel fresh which can easily be accomplished in the kitchen sink. Winter van life makes outdoor showers practically impossible unless you have an amazing water heater or love a polar bear plunge.

Even people with full shower facilities don't shower every day because of the aggressive water consumption. They'd be filling their tanks three times a week to keep up with the demand. The couple we know with the recirculating shower has to dump and fill that tank weekly to stop soap build up (plus I don't trust a shower you can't pee in).

After a month or so of adjustment you'll realize that your hair doesn't actually get all that greasy by day 2. These days I can go 4 or 5 days without a proper shower and feel pretty good. If needed, I take pits and ditch showers over the sink or use wet wipes and I'm good to go.

Plus, there's nothing more amazing than having a hot shower after a long stretch without one. It really makes you appreciate how amazing a shower is and how precious water is as well.

Where to Get Your Mail

If you don't have a stationary home, what is your home address? Where will your bills be addressed to and how will the government reach you? These are all sensible questions with very easy answers.

Our home address is actually Frankie's mom's place. He and his siblings bought her the house after their father passed away and so since leaving New York, it has become our home base.

Right now we are building out our new rig there. It acts as our official mailing address as well. When we're on the road, Frankie's mom will have a look at any mail that comes in for us and let us know if it looks important. Most of the time it's junk or flyers as we've opted to receive all our bills and statements electronically. If it looks official or important, she will send us a photo of it.

Of course, not everyone has a super awesome mom like Frankie does and so they don't have an address to use.

If you truly don't have anyone, a family member or close friend, whose address you can use, you can get a PO box. These come with a small monthly fee but work for just about everything when it comes to mail, however some government forms might require a physical address.

While traveling you can also have the post office redirect the contents of your PO box to a more convenient location. While this option is great for regular letters, it's not so good for receiving large packages or shipments. PO boxes are quite small.

There are also services you can pay for that will give you an address to ship everything too. They will open and scan copies of your mail to you and will store bigger packages for a designated timeframe. The most popular is www.virtualmailbox.com but there are a many to choose from with differing service packages and rates.

If you'd rather not pay a monthly fee but only as needed, have your items shipped to a UPS Store. This works for packages and deliveries you might need on the road, not as your full-time address.

Find the nearest UPS Store, put their address on your delivery with your name on it, and voila. Once it's delivered you show up at the store with your ID and pay $5 per package. I would call the store before shipping anything to them just to make sure there's nothing more you need to do.

Some stores want you to be on a list before they will accept your package but most don't care at all. They will hold any package for a month or more before sending it back. Post offices generally have a similar service, just call ahead to find out what the requirements are at each location.

Another great option for random purchases on the road is Amazon lockers. These are mainly located in more populated areas and Whole Foods locations (Whole Foods has great free Wi-Fi by the way). When checking out on Amazon.com simply select the locker in the area you want to collect your package at. Just make sure it's selectable and that you don't type in the address We did that the first time and did not get our package unfortunately.

And the final low-tech option is to have all your packages sent to the next friend's place you know you're going to be visiting. We'll ask Frankie's mom to pack up all our mail and send it to that friend so that when we arrive there, it's like Christmas morning opening up everything.

As with all problems one can come up with for living van life, there's a pretty easy solution. Designate a friend, family member, or paid service as your home address for all your regular mail and government correspondence, then have packages and other deliveries sent to the nearest UPS Store or Post Office. Simple as that.

In over a year on the road we've never had any trouble getting mail or deliveries.

Laundry

Another reality of van life is that laundry is going to pile up. Very quickly you will realize that it's better to wear the same shirt twice than to have it fill your laundry basket. The laundry basket is an often-overlooked aspect of the van build layout.

This is an unfortunate oversight when you've got a 20-pound bag with nowhere to go but your open floor space. Now you've got a laundry filled bean-bag-chair, dope.

Having a large enough cavern for you to drop your dirty clothes in is a must. It's also a must that you realize your clothes are not as dirty as you think. Pants can be re-worn many times before they need to be washed. If you're not going commando, those bad boys haven't touched anything that would make them dirty (unless you have a spill or go for some extreme workout).

In most homes there's a chair, hook, or equally forgotten area where half dirty clothes live. You wore them once so they aren't dirty enough to go in the bin, but you're too lazy or don't want to put them away with your 100% clean clothes. In a van, this isn't really an option.

Just one item out of place and your whole living quarters look like a mess. Perhaps I'm just a neat freak, although I'm really not, but in this tiny space, even a stray sock can make your home feel like a complete pigsty.

Once you resign yourself to the fact, you'll be wearing the same clothes over and over again, you'll need to develop a system to store the not quite clean items. Because there's no place for an extra half worn clothes chair, you really just have to put them away between wears.

Perhaps all the half dirty stuff has its own bin or it all goes away inside out so you can easily identify it when you do go to do laundry. Whatever your system, keep your home tidy by giving even your dirty clothes a place.

The physical practice of doing laundry is quite easy. Anytime you visit friends or family take advantage of the free washer and dryer and put in a load. On the road, a quick google search will find you many laundry mats in towns and cities of all sizes.

Stash your quarters and small bills so you always have some on hand and always bring your own detergent as the stuff they sell at the laundry mat is almost always overpriced or of poor quality.

If you're one of those people who can't be bothered to fold and put away your laundry when you're done with it, many laundry mats will wash and fold your clothes for you, generally charging by the pound, so you don't even have to worry about that.

Storing and doing laundry is just another unavoidable life chore that needs to be taken care of on the road. No matter how hard you try to avoid it, you have to *adult* once in a while.

"Whenever you go on a trip to visit foreign lands or distant places, remember that they are all someone's home and backyard." — Vera Nazarian

Leave No Trace Principals

As you make your way around the globe, you'll quickly realize that your tiny garbage can fills up very quickly. You'll also notice that big bulky packaging has nowhere to live once you're done with it (plus big food purchases probably won't even fit in your fridge!).

Just like how you minimized the things you had; you also need to minimize the garbage you create and the environmental footprint you leave behind.

A few weeks ago, we shared a camp spot we love near Bend, Oregon with our virtual community. We received some backlash for sharing a spot online because "other vanlifers would come and destroy it". While I'm sure there are a few bad eggs out there, most of the vanlifers I've met care deeply about the planet.

It's hard not to when your backyard is an ever-changing scene of natural beauty. It would be such a shame to leave trash behind and spoil a beautiful scenic location.

Frankie and I do our best to practice the leave no trace principals. When we leave a location, we want to leave it exactly the same or better than we found it. We often pick-up trash left by others. It might not be our trash but it is our planet. The last thing we want is to give vanlifers a bad name and I hope you feel the same.

Some cities experiencing a homelessness crisis don't want people living in their cars and a big reason is that many of these people don't follow the leave no trace principals I'm about to explain.

Sure, not all of them are guilty of littering, but those few bad eggs all crammed together in tight proximity make a bad name for everyone. It would be an absolute shame if more and more places put pressure on vanlifers because a few don't know how or can't be bothered to clean up after themselves.

The leave no trace principals that all who travel into the wild should follow are:

1. **Plan Ahead and Prepare**: For vanlifers this means make sure you have enough water, food and fuel on board for however long you're planning on camping out.
2. **Travel and Camp on Durable Surfaces**: That means don't drive your rig through a beautiful untouched meadow. Stick to roads and camp on hard surfaces (this will help you not get stuck too).

3. **Dispose of Waste Properly**: Take all your trash, recycling, and compost out with you and find a real garbage/recycling can for it. Don't burry it or try to burn it in the camp fire.
4. **Leave What You Find**: Don't build any structures or dig random holes you don't fill in. You are not Bear Grylls trying to survive in the wilderness, you live in a tiny home. This also means don't carve your name into rocks or trees and don't take the natural flora with you when you go, even just one flower.
5. **Minimize Campfire Impacts**: With the craziest wild fire seasons the West Coast has seen in years, we should all know that fire is not something to be messed around with. Build it small and safe. Put it out completely when you're done.
6. **Respect Wildlife**: It's their home, we're just visiting.
7. **Be Considerate of Other Visitors**: Make it fun for everyone to get out and camp. Be friendly. Be courteous. Be quiet. Especially now with COVID give way for others walking on the trails.

The longer we live in a van, the more we are moving towards renewable and everlasting products that won't fill our garbage cans and pollute the world. We've replaced plastic sandwich bags with reusable silicone.

We limit plastic shopping bags at the grocery store because as our home and whole kitchen is in the parking lot, we just take the cart right outside and unload it into the van (it is handy to have a few plastic bags around – reuse them before you toss them).

We always separate our recyclables because they are big and bulky and would fill our garbage can in a minute. We never use plastic utensils or paper plates because our whole kitchen and dishwashing station is right here.

We are moving towards a zero-waste lifestyle as best we can, not only because it's amazing for the planet but it's also better for the small confines of living in a van. That's part of the reason why we're moving towards a more plant based, vegan lifestyle as well. It's tricky to have meat and dairy products in a fridge that might trip and warm significantly because of low solar power.

It's also tricky to fully wash and avoid cross contamination between your cooking dishes when you have such a small workspace (and potentially no hot water). We feel better, lighter and have much better digestion when we take meat and dairy products from our diet. This is another way we are leaving a smaller foot print on the planet.

Reducing your environmental footprint is good not only for the planet but for you as a person as well. You will feel so much more fulfilled when you've cleaned up a campsite someone else trashed then being the person doing the trashing. Karma is very important on the road so be sure to always do your part so that when you're in need of a hand, there's one ready to reach out and help.

"It is our collective and individual responsibility … to preserve and tend to the world in which we all live." — Dalai Lama

Breakdowns

Engine issues suck. That's true whether you live in your vehicle or not. Engine issues when your home is your van, really suck. If your van has to be in the shop for 2 weeks, where will you go? What happens when you're driving along in the middle of nowhere and the engine just dies?

Even with a brand-new van and even if you've spent hours, days, or months working on your rig laying a strong foundation, at some point, you will have a breakdown. Once, for example, Frankie and I were parked in a grocery store parking lot waiting for the mechanics in a small town on the coast of Oregon to open on a Monday morning.

A tiny component that pushes our brake fluid to the back tires was totally kaput so we couldn't even drive to the next town or the beach around the corner without putting our lives and home seriously at risk. Monday we could order the part but then who knew how long we would be stuck in this parking lot. When said part did arrive, the job took no more than a few hours and we were on our way.

This was not the first time we found ourselves broken-down. Once in Jackson Hole, we woke up on a frigidly cold morning to find our engine wouldn't start. Frankie noticed one of the engine fans was held on by only 1 out of the required 3 screws. After we fixed that and the van finally started, we headed south to Salt Lake City where we knew we had a friend's house to park at.

We shipped the other required parts to their home and then installed them ourselves. While all this was going on, we spent almost two weeks parked in our friend's driveway not wanting to drive anywhere for fear of further damaging the engine.

Hopefully, you have some general knowledge about your engine so that you can fix little issues that might slow you down. For example, we were driving along and all of a sudden, we heard this crazy whooshing screaming noise coming from the engine.

We pulled over right away and popped the hood. Because Frankie knows his way around our engine, he was quickly able to see that an air hose had popped off. He put it back on, secured it with a clamp, and we were on our way.

This could have been a costly issue had he not been able to identify the issue himself. We might have needed a tow or diagnostics from a mechanic. Instead, five minutes later we were back on the road for free.

If you're able to do the work yourself, there are many DIY garages where, for a fee, you can use their lifts and tools. The one we've been to many times that costs $30/hour versus a mechanic that can charge upwards of $150 an hour so it's definitely a money saver. The only downside is that you usually get dirty and have to do the work yourself.

You should familiarize yourself with parts websites online so you can look up the items you need to replace and have a rough estimate of the cost of those parts before going to the mechanic. Most shops upcharge parts so if you can bring your own and just have them install it, you can save money.

Maybe Frankie is just hypervigilant, but I've spent more time at auto parts stores in the last two years than I did my entire life beforehand – I can't say that it's been thrilling.

If you do end up in a spot where you need to leave your vehicle behind at a mechanics shop, you will have to pack a bag and find a new home for a few days. This might be with friends or family, an Airbnb, couch surfing or at a hotel. Your insurance might cover a rental car for a few days.

You should also check how far your insurance will tow you. Some plans only tow up to 50 miles which could leave you with a costly tow from the middle of nowhere.

We were lucky both times we broke down because we were able to stay in the van the duration of the breakdown. That's good news because it means we didn't have to get a hotel room or Airbnb for the night. It means we could stay in our home and not worry about it being at a mechanic for days on end.

If you are ever in that position, you'll have to essentially move out of your home, empty the refrigerator of perishables, grab clothes and toiletries, perhaps stash valuables and find a place to stay.

The one time we left Lolo with a mechanic overnight it was near my parents' home. The diesel mechanic (a bit harder to find and sometimes more expensive because of their expertise over gasoline vehicle mechanics) had come highly recommended by a family member so we knew our baby was in safe hands.

Luckily, we had a place to stay and even a borrowed car to get us to and from the mechanic. It didn't matter how many days they held the vehicle because we were safe and sound at my parents' home, no bookings to extend or new accommodations needed. Our plumbing did freeze during that time though because it was in the dead of winter and our heater was off the entire time it was with him. You win some you lose some.

Breakdowns are why having an emergency stash of cash is so important. You have no control over how your vehicle is going to operate and sometimes, especially when you put so many miles on her fast with a heavy build in the back, she's going to have mechanical issues. Even if you do all the regular maintenance you're supposed to, anything can go wrong. You need to have money available to pay for repairs and any additional accommodations you might need while she's being fixed.

I've not heard of a mechanic yet that would allow a person to live in a vehicle in their shop. Most of them won't even let you sit in the van while they work. An overnight in their shop would be a whole lot of trust for them to allow you to sleep in the same space as all their tools and I'm sure there's got to be some kind of liability issues.

Perhaps they would be okay with you staying in a back-parking lot or something similar but who knows. We slept on the street outside a mechanic shop once because we got towed there around 10pm the night before and couldn't move. It was not ideal in terms of scenery or smell but very convenient that we were able to get our rig fixed first thing the next morning.

You should know off the top of your head what to do or who to call when something goes wrong.

- What does your insurance cover?
- Do you have an additional roadside assistance plan like AAA/CAA?
- Do you have a bag of tools in the back so that you can fix little issues as they arise?
- Do you have a warranty on the vehicle?
- What does that warranty cover?
- Do you have an emergency fund to cover any unexpected engine issue bills?
- Safety cones on board if you need to steer away other drivers?
- Tools on board and knowledge of your engine to help you get back on the road if possible?
- Do you have a heating source like a candle if your power goes out and you're stranded?

- What about a jack in case you need to change a tire?

You need to have an action plan for what to do in case something goes wrong. Hopefully, nothing ever does go wrong with your engine. In my original budget I didn't have any significant money set aside for engine repairs. I built in an extra $50 per month for all things maintenance. But our first month on the road we had a $350 bill from a mechanic.

I had this idea that once the van was built and we were on the road, that's it, we're done! Now we just get to travel and enjoy. What I didn't realize that all that traveling and enjoying meant we were putting a lot of miles on an old van that hadn't been driven like that in quite some time. There were bound to be issues and we've paid for all of them whether in time or in cash. So be prepared to do the same, you never know.

We truly believe that, you are where you are, when you are, on purpose. If you've been stranded in some random town, it's for a reason. Perhaps the delay will link you up perfectly with another vanlifer down the road. Maybe while you're in that town you find the most delicious brewery and help support the local economy by eating there every day.

Or just maybe, you find the perfect puppy to adopt at the local shelter, that's what happened to us. Now we're a duo plus a wonderful puppy named Paco who spent his first 2 days with us waiting to get our brakes fixed.

Yes, we were stuck living in a grocery store parking lot for a while but were pretty content. We had unlimited food and water plus no stress about money because of our emergency savings – and our brand-new to us puppy. We bought an older van and knew there would be times when we would need to slow down to get her fixed, it's all par for the course. For our second rig, we went with something newer and more reliable so that we would have less breakdowns and time in the shop.

But there are no guarantees in van life, even $100,000 rigs can breakdown.

Earn Money to Extend Travel

Whether you saved a boat load of money or not, you will eventually arrive at a juncture where your bank account will force you to decide: do I keep traveling or do I settle down? If you decide to keep traveling, you'll have to pick up work to reload your bank account so you can continue to enjoy your nomad life.

Perhaps you have a particular set of skills you can put to work. Frankie, for example, is trained as a heating and air conditioning technician. He could pick up work anywhere because he has a skill and had the foresight to bring the tools of his trade on board with us.

I on the other hand, spent a decade as an Executive Assistant. While this is a wonderful profession and was very lucrative in New York City after climbing the corporate ladder for years, it isn't the type of work I would want to pick up in some random town for minimum wage.

I on the other hand, spent a decade as an Executive Assistant. While this is a wonderful profession and was very lucrative in New York City after climbing the corporate ladder for years, it isn't the type of work I would want to pick up in some random town for minimum wage. It would be much more lucrative for me, and provide a more flexible work arrangement, to work in the restaurant or hospitality world.

Bartending or waitressing is a great way to make cash quickly, just find a busy restaurant in need of an extra pair of hands. I do have prior experience in this field having worked my way through college as a waitress. I found waitressing a fun profession that quickly lined my pockets.

There's also the lucrative business of seasonal work. You can drive yourself to exactly where you need to be to pick up jobs only available and plentiful at certain times of the year. Perhaps you want to work at music festivals all summer, be a ski instructor all winter, help with the fall pumpkin harvest or relive your youth as a summer camp counselor.

Maybe you're great with numbers and want to help people complete their taxes, or you want to do something more physically challenging and to work as a logger in Alaska.

If you can drive yourself there, get ready to make use of unlimited resources both locally and online to help you find a seasonal gig that will refill your pockets and allow you to travel longer.

While you're working, it's imperative to actually save money. Even if you're spending a few bucks to eat, drink and enjoy yourself, you should still be putting 40-50% of your take home pay into the bank. If you truly want to save to travel, you need to be frugal while you're earning so you can make it last when you're not.

With your housing costs covered (you live in a van after all) your daily expenses should be quite low. The worst thing you can do is spend too much and get yourself stuck because you can't afford to go anywhere else.

How to make money on the road is one of the most asked questions in the van life groups. Hopefully you took my advice in prior chapters and built up your savings before hitting the road or perhaps you'll take a page from the next chapter and become a digital nomad, or maybe you'll be a rock star and do it all.

To save you time searching, here are a list of ways that actual vanlifers make money on the road (not digitally). It's a long one:

- Dog Walker
- Restaurant/hospitality industry service worker
- Traveling massage therapist

- Handyman worker
- Use your existing trade such as HVAC and offer service calls
- Craft maker/seller
- Metal detector on beach to find treasure
- Grocery delivery
- Food delivery
- Stuff delivery
- Amazon package delivery
- Sell old stuff/flip consignment items
- Babysitter
- House sitter
- Temp agency office work
- Find cool items and sell them yard sale style
- Drive for Google maps type companies
- Wedding, event, nature or photographer of any kind
- Sell drone footage
- Camp site host
- Seasonal work (forestry, gift wrapping, farming, campground work, tourism, etc.)
- Van building for others
- Handyman on Craigs List
- All types of gigs on Craigs List
- Forage for mushrooms/antlers/cool rocks
- Childcare
- House sitting
- Exotic dancer
- Phone sex operator

There are so many apps and websites that can connect you with this type of work. Want to dog walk? Get Wag. Want to babysit? Download care.com. The great thing about this day and age is that the world is at the tip of your fingers.

You are not the first person ever to look for work and because there are so many people in the same boat, there are limitless resources to help. If you prefer an offline approach, you can always ask locals, look at physical job boards or walk into restaurants/stores and offer your resume.

This mentality of work to travel, travel some more, runout of money, work, then travel again is sustainable for a few years. In my opinion, this lifestyle won't be helping your retirement savings or long-term goals of buying a home/land/bigger rig or any of those other *adult* pursuits. Of course, who knows, maybe the longer you travel the more you will find yourself and what you're truly meant to do.

Maybe you'll have an epiphany and create the next Amazon – maybe you'll hit the lotto jackpot! Anything is possible, but if you really want to make a living as a traveler, I believe becoming a digital nomad is your best bet. This way you can earn money all the time, not just when you stop for a while. You could also do a combination of both digital and non-digital to get the best of both worlds.

Before we left the security of our jobs, making money on the road was a major worry for me. What if we went broke? I had never not had a job for an extended period of time and was struggling with losing the security that brought, a paycheck you could count on every two weeks. If you have figured me out by now, I did the most sensible thing I could come up with, I made a list. A giant list of all the ways I could come up with to make money while traveling. I let my imagination run wild and came up with things as mundane as picking up coins on the street to the wild and highly unlikely possibility of Frankie becoming an exotic dancer (he'd be better at it than I would). When I was finished with the list, I realized that no matter what, we would be able to make money somehow.

We had our nest egg and a whole host of ways to help it grow. Just seeing all the options laid out on paper put my mind at ease. We are both highly skilled, personable, smart people who can do just about anything. How to make money isn't something we need to worry about, we just have to decide how we want to make it – and I'm guessing the same is true for you. There are unlimited ways to earn cash, you just have to choose your favorite.

It feels like I've dedicated a lot of this book to money so if that's not your bag, I apologize. For me, money equals stability and security. Even when my backyard changes every day, even when the foods I'm eating vary from region to region, even when the van breaks down and we need repairs, I know we're safe because we have money in the bank and many ways to make more of it.

"What we really want to do is what we are really meant to do. When we do what we are meant to do, money comes to us, doors open for us, we feel useful, and the work we do feels like play to us." — Julia Cameron

Become a Digital Nomad

Welcome to the 21st century. With the internet all things are possible. You can without a doubt make a career for yourself online that will more than pay for your nomadic tendencies. Many companies are happy to have functions preformed remotely (even more so in our post COVID world) or you can create your own empire. If you're tech savvy, the options for digital work are endless and you can tailor these to suit your skills.

To do this successfully, you will need reliable internet which we'll discuss in the next chapter. You will also need to decide what kind of schedule you want to keep while working. Do you want something very flexible so that you can work whenever you want? Or would you rather something that is the same time every day? Can you commit to a full-time gig or would you prefer something that allows for more adventure on the road? If you're entrepreneurially minded, how many hours is it going to take to get your venture off the ground and generate income? The amount of money you need might dictate how many hours you work. No matter how many hours you want to commit to working, you can find jobs that suit your lifestyle.

Here are a few options for digital work that only require internet connection:
- English teacher
- Virtual tutor
- Call center customer service
- Virtual assistant
- Virtual ad manager
- Affiliate marketing
- Drop shipping
- Amazon wholesale/affiliate links
- Copywriting
- Graphic design
- Coder/programmer/website designer
- Ghost writer
- Blogger/Influencer with large following
- YouTube videos with lots of views
- Online surveys
- Investing/day trading
- Digital marketer
- Social media manager
- Selling crafts or thrift items online
- Writing eBooks
- Proofreading
- Voice overs
- Selling photographs or videos as stock art
- Remote office work
- Any corporate job that's 100% remote

I'm literally just scratching the surface here. The possibilities for online work are endless. If you prefer the self-employed route, the options are only limited by your imagination. Proponents of the 4 Hour Work Week will tell you, it's easy to make tons of money working online. This is for sure true, but success is unlikely to occur overnight. Yes, the dream of having a sales funnel that makes you millions in your sleep is achievable but trust me, those people are putting a lot of work into their sales funnels (at least until they have it all figured out). The nice thing is you can put the work in when you want to not when your boss tells you to. The tricky thing is being motivated enough every day to put the work in without a boss telling you to.

Same is true for those of us trying to make a living as *influencers*. Of course, there are stories of YouTubers who go viral with their first video. They are guaranteed a consistent income from YouTube no matter what they put out because they've got millions of eyeballs on their videos. The more eyeballs aka views, the more money. But more likely, your trajectory will be more gradual like mine, Frankie's and so many others, a long and slow road.

As of this writing, there are about 4,210,000,000 search results for van life on the internet. That includes millions of YouTube videos most with meager views and hardly any following. There are only a few standout accounts really making money. You likely already know these because you've seen their content in your quest to learn everything about van life. These chosen few (chosen by *the people* and search algorithms) can drop videos that get over 100,000 views per week.

For reference, YouTube pays about $3-5 per 1,000 views. So, if you've built up a channel that's getting 100,000 new views/week plus probably another 500,000 views a month from old videos still showing up in search results, you can make between $3,000 and $5,000 a month. I could certainly live van life with that kind of income.

For a very long time my channel (which I started 3 years before van life) was making about $50 a month. In the short time we've switched over to van life content, the views and cash have gone up significantly. I've also had full time hours to put into the channel.

Frankie and I combined efforts and went from producing one video a week to three a week plus spending hours promoting them all, replying to comments and interacting with brands. When I was working a fulltime job, I didn't have the bandwidth to give my channel which is probably why it didn't grow. Now that I'm taking it as seriously as a full-time job, it's growing.

At this point I don't know if this growth is sustainable or if it's a blip. Can I count on this newfound $2,000 per month or should I consider this an exceptionally good month that will eventually go back down? Only time will tell. For now, I'm happy with the extra cash in my pocket as it means that our expenses on the road are covered for the month. Every month we make over $1,000 on YouTube is another month we get to travel and enjoy van life. Of course, it would be great to make enough money to travel, save and invest - all in good time.

The hope is that Frankie and I will achieve success on YouTube (if you want to help out come on over and subscribe! www.youtube.com/fnavanlife) but there's no guarantee of that. We enjoy making videos and from the very beginning have said that if this whole YouTube thing takes off and we can make a living doing that, fantastic. If not, we've got savings in the bank and skills that can get us jobs elsewhere.

I think this is the mindset with which you should approach all digital nomad endeavors. If you can't say for sure you're going to get paid a certain amount of money for a certain amount of work, don't count on it. All entrepreneurial pursuits come with inherent risk. I would hate for you to quit your job, move into a van and expect to start making millions selling widgets on Amazon next week (if that does happen you should definitely write a book about it because I would read that!).

Trading time for money is the surest, if not slightly less sexy, way to earn an income. Oh, did I neglect to mention that entrepreneurship generally requires a huge number of work-for-free hours to make potentially nothing? Frankie and I spend countless hours editing and promoting our videos on social platforms. If I was getting paid by the hour, I'd be making pennies right now! I'm really raining on the entrepreneur train which is wild considering I am one myself – maybe I'm just not a very good one!

Heck even in writing this book I'm wondering how many hours I'm devoting and how much I will end up making in the end. My last Amazon book about administrative support currently brings in about $20 a month. It would take like 200 months making that to recoup my time at only $20/hour.

We love to support other vanlifers who make beautiful things to share with the world. Our logo was designed by a fellow vanlifer from Germany. We've shared van builds from many different vanlifers to help promote their brands and are starting to feature fellow vanlifers in our live chats. I'm always on the lookout for ways to help our community however we can. I know from meeting many vanlifers on the road and online that all of us who have chosen this lifestyle dream similar dreams so I want to support them in theirs.

If you'd like to connect with us on Instagram, DM @fnavanlife and we'll happily support your account. If you have a YouTube channel, comment on one of our videos and we'll follow you back. If we're in the same area and you want us to film your van tour to share your story with our audience, reach out. We'd love to meet up and share stories about our shared passions.

However, you decide to make money online, the possibilities are literally endless. Know that a little hard work, perseverance, creativity and intrinsic motivation go a long way. You will find a way to make money on the road, you might just have to try a few options first before landing on the gig that works perfectly for you.

"You can only become truly accomplished at something you love. Don't make money your goal. Instead, pursue the things you love doing, and then do them so well that people can't take their eyes off you." — Maya Angelou

Finding Internet

If you're going to be working from the road or if you just want to download an entire season of Tiny Home Nation on Netflix, you're going to need internet. Wi-Fi is available in many public places because, much like toilets, everyone needs it. And just like toilets, finding free Wi-Fi has become trickier now that COVID has closed many public places. It's still possible to find it but depending on what state you're in, establishments might not be allowing people to sit inside.

We tried to go to a coffee shop the other day but their inside was completely closed, they were drive through only and you couldn't even use the bathroom. We have been known to sit in parking lots of places with free Wi-Fi because sometimes the signal is strong enough to reach the van so it doesn't matter if it's open or closed.

Hopefully in the coming months/years things will go back to normal and these ways of siphoning internet will all flow freely again. Here's a list of places to get public Wi-Fi (if it's a small business, you should definitely buy something when you're there):

- Coffee shops
- Restaurants
- Libraries

- Internet Cafes
- Hotel lobbies
- Museums
- Airports
- Some public transportation hubs
- Grocery stores
- Cruise around a neighborhood looking for open networks
- Use apps like WifiMap or Wifi Free Spot to find connections
- Use your cell phone as a mobile hot spot

If you're going to be sitting in any establishment for a prolonged period of time using their free Wi-Fi, know that this comes with a cost. You really should purchase something as a thanks for the bandwidth. Whether that's a cup of coffee or a lunch special, it's the right thing to do. It's also very important to tip your server, who knows, they might be saving for their own van life adventure.

If you don't have enough money to buy something and tip, choose a location for Wi-Fi, like the library, where paid patronage isn't expected. Or see if you can get their Wi-Fi from the street so you're not taking up a paying customer's seat.

Having a VPN is a smart way to protect yourself on these public networks. The VPN routes your internet connection through their own private server instead of yours which makes it harder for people to hack into your computer. Because you're on a public network, there's a possibility someone else on that network will be up to no good. A VPN will help protect you.

The benefit of these Wi-Fi options is that they are free. The downside is that there's no guarantee of speed, reliability or accessibility. Many public networks allow quick surfing and downloads but limit upload speeds drastically. We've been on networks that will only upload 1% of a YouTube video in an hour when on a home network the whole video would upload in 30 minutes. If you're just trying to check in with friends and family on Facebook or read the news, these free networks are more than adequate, especially when you also have a cell phone with a data plan. If you're trying to work remotely or upload/download large files, you can't count on free sources.

To create your own Wi-Fi signal in your van, there are a few options. The first and easiest is the mobile hot spot. Depending on your cell phone plan, you might be able to link up to the data on your phone so you can use internet on your other devices. We had T-Mobile which gave us unlimited hot spot connections included in our monthly $60 each plan. The downside was that T-Mobile's coverage area is limited compared to other carriers and even though our hot spot was unlimited, it started to buffer speeds after a certain number of megabytes.

We recently switched to Verizon for better coverage but are definitely paying more for that luxury. Because we work full time on the road, we need a reliable cell phone connection. Many vanlifers get into van life to disconnect so being without service for days wouldn't be a big deal, in fact it might be exactly what they want. But for us, it's imperative to get online.

Shop around between cellphone carriers for the best deal as some carriers charge heavily for hotspot usage. You'll also want to think about roaming and international fees as you may find yourself in areas not covered by your network. It would be a real pain to end up with an insanely expensive cellphone bill because you didn't look into it before you drove to Costa Rica.

As I mentioned, the downside with very cheap cellphone plans is that the coverage area is limited. We would often pull up the coverage map to see which towns we'd get the best service in and head there between days off-grid. Big cities are always covered but out in the wilderness, it's a crapshoot. We did have a T-Mobile specific signal booster which would turn 1 bar of service into 4, but if there's no service, there's no service.

After traveling with other nomads for a while, it was clear that our provider was the problem as they surfed the net no problem while we had zero connection.

WeBoost and SureCall are cell phone single boosters that work much like the free one we got from our carrier (most carriers will give you one for free if you complain about service at your home – they will tell you they only work in one location but from our experience that's not true).

These vehicle specific boosters come with a hefty price tag starting around $500. But again, if you have no bars of service, you have no service to boost so this isn't really helpful when going completely off-grid.

Most cell phone companies sell mobile internet plans. These work as additional hot spots either through your phone or a secondary device. You're still tapping into the cellular networks though so again you might not always have coverage. The secondary devices can be mounted to your vehicle, sim card inserted and voila, you've created your own Wi-Fi network inside your van for about $700 upfront and your monthly internet bill. The benefit of these is that they come with a powerful antenna that will find a signal well beyond what you cell phone can locate. It's also smart to get an alternate carrier for the booster so that if your Verizon service isn't working, your AT&T Wi-Fi antenna might pick up an alternate signal.

For some people internet really isn't a big deal. The whole reason they do van life is to get away from technology and simply enjoy nature. We have friends who will go completely off-grid for weeks with no cellphone or anything and be perfectly happy. We are not those people. For us, our livelihood depends on the internet and so sometimes we have to make our plans around when we're going to have service. We can really only be off grid for a day or two before we feel like we need to get back to civilization. Just like all other aspects of van life, how you want to set up your connection to the world, is completely up to your needs, preferences and budget.

Night Driving

It's always best to drive in the daytime, but sometimes night driving is unavoidable. Of course, in some countries, night driving should be avoided completely no matter what. In Central America for example, where the quality of roads is questionable and the likelihood of untoward activity increases between dusk and dawn, you'd be a fool to drive at night. In Canada and the US though, especially when the sun sets at 4:30pm in the middle of winter, you will often find yourself driving in complete darkness to arrive somewhere by 7:00pm.

Because of our goal to visit 71 mountains in 4 months, we often had to drive in complete darkness to arrive at a mountain in the middle of the night, just to wake up and ride in the morning. Hopefully you're cruising at a more relaxed pace because we often wondered about all the beautiful scenery we missed by not being able to see beyond our headlights.

No matter where you're going, driving at night is inherently more dangerous. Your visibility is reduced. You can be blinded by oncoming lights. You might be surprised by an obstacle in the middle of the road, a pot hole or an animal. You have to stay alert. Unfortunately, straining to see past those bright headlights will make your eyes more tired. You can try yellow tinted glasses to help with this. I find them very useful to block the glare of oncoming lights no matter how uncool I look.

Another safety device you should consider are deer whistles. When driving in the wee hours especially in rural places, it is more likely that an animal will jump out into the road, potentially causing an accident. These deer whistles, mounted to the hood of your car, make a noise that is inaudible to you but acts as a warning to animals not to come close. After a few close calls, we installed ours and noticed instead of coming out to the road, animals would stay well back at the tree line.

When driving at night, some areas will be very well lit and others basically pitch black. High beams are a must but please be kind to other drivers. Never ever drive behind someone with your brights on. The person at the front of the convoy is the only car who should be using their high beams. If you've got your brights on too, they are reflecting off the driver's mirrors directly into their eyes. If you're driving along in the dark and see a car coming towards you from the distance, please turn off your brights before you're directly in front of them. Basically, as soon as you see the other car you should shut off your brights. This is just a common curtesy that apparently not many drivers seem to be aware of or adhere to. We've been blinded way too many times. Thanks for letting me get that off my chest!

The one great big plus of driving at night is that there is virtually no traffic. If you know you're driving though a big city and not stopping, it could be best to do this at night when no one is around instead of in the middle of the day or at rush hour. The downside is that you'll find many stores, restaurants and even gas stations closed.

Fill up before it gets too late especially if you're somewhere more rural because you might just find the next gas station shut their pumps off at 11:00pm and even if it's 11:01pm they can't turn them back on (that happened to us once in Vermont). Make sure you have food or snacks because likewise your opportunities for buying food decrease. And in case of a breakdown, you should always have a safety light or cone, a heat source (ours is a diesel heater but we also have lots of candles just in case) and warm clothes in your van - but you live in there so likely you'll already have that sorted out.

Driving at night is almost as dangerous as driving at sunrise or sunset when the sun is directly in your line of sight. We will generally get off the road and have dinner to avoid these times of day as statistically that's when most accidents happen (we are rarely up before sunrise so no worries there).

No matter what time of day you're driving, you need to be smart. Stay well back of the vehicle in front of you and don't make any sudden moves.

Your van will be heavy and slower to stop meaning that if you're too close or something jumps out into the road, you don't have much time to react at all. You have to be vigilant and drive with the utmost care. Your entire home in your van so driving it carefully is a must. If that means you get off the road and finish the drive tomorrow, so be it.

"Opportunity is missed by most people because it is dressed in overalls and looks like work." — Thomas Edison

Regular Maintenance

Vans are a lot of work. Your home is constantly giggling, moving, and swaying from side to side. Nuts, bolts, clamps, and couplings are going to come loose. If you're not checking these things over from time to time, you might end up with a bigger problem on your hands. Like how we didn't realize a plumbing connection had come loose and ended up with a flood. Or when we didn't realize two of the three screws holding on our engine fan had disappeared.

It's smart to do a full walk around of your vehicle each day to look for anything unusual. One day we found a whole panel above the tire was just flapping in the wind. If we didn't catch that right away, it might have just blown right off never to be found again. Another day we realized that our tire had gone flat overnight. You never know, there could be a kid under your van or a possum might have crawled into the engine! A quick scan of your vehicle makes sure that everything is in safe and in top shape before you get driving and helps avoid a minor situation from becoming much worse.

There are several other tasks you need to think about every few weeks or months to ensure you have a smooth-running machine and home on your hands.

I've put together the list below to help you start thinking about regular maintenance items and checks you need to be doing on your van.
Engine:
- Oil changes (check vehicle manual for mileage requirements)
- Transition fluid check and replace (check vehicle manual for mileage requirements)
- Fuel filter change
- Check fluids regularly (coolant/windshield wiper/oil/rear and front differential/brake/power steering – there are A LOT of fluids!)
- Check tire pressure
- Tire balance (is your steering wheel pulling in a certain direction while driving?)
- Check tires for wear on tread, especially if wear is uneven as this could indicate they are unbalanced or have unequal pressure
- Air filters for vehicle intake and air conditioning
- Ensure there is no rust or build up on your main car battery connection points
- Listen for any unusual noises and investigate where they are coming from
- Look under the car after it's been parked for any leaking fluids

- Check clamps on hoses to ensure they are tight/not slipping
- Wash the body of the car especially if you've been somewhere very dusty like a playa or icy where salty roads are present

Van Build:
- Water filters
- Electrical connections (these can jiggle loose)
- Clean off solar panels (snow, dust, dirt buildup, ice, etc.)
- Cleaning vents/fans
- Tightening bolts and screws
- Check all doors to ensure there is no corrosion of the seals

Each build will have unique things that need checking depending on its components, but this list should get you started. But I get it, all this work might seem exhausting when you're ready to just sit on the beach with a cold beer in your hand.

The fact of the matter is that you haven't just bought yourself a van, you've bought yourself a big heavy house on wheels. Just like you would need to learn how to change the air filters in your home air conditioning system, you need to figure it out in your van as well. Sure, you can just pay someone to take care of all this instead of you. But once you learn how to change your own oil, you'll never pay someone else to do it for you again.

A friend recently described a van build as if you're building a home that goes through an earthquake every day from driving it around. After an earthquake you'd do a quick walk around your house right? Your van build requires the same attention.

Tools You Need

You do not necessarily need everything on this list but you really should have a set of tools on board. These items will help with regular maintenance as well as in case of emergency. Even if you don't think you'll be doing the work yourself, they could come in handy for someone else working on your van like if a good Samaritan comes along when you're stranded but doesn't have any tools, good thing you've got a set.

Plus, you'll save yourself a whole lot of time and money if you can replace or fix things on your own and keep up with general maintenance. Even if your vehicle is still under warranty, that warranty does not include everything you built in the back.

- Tire pressure gauge to the correct PSI for your tires
- Rags to check oil/fluids
- Basic electrical meter
- Screw driver set
- Nut driver set
- Socket set
- Serpentine belt remover
- Breaker bar
- A supply of all those fluids we mentioned above so you can replace/top them up

- Pliers
- Torque wrench
- Oil drain pan (if you're going to change it yourself)
- Latex gloves (so you don't get greasy while you work)
- A work light/flash light/headlight
- Hand cleaning solution for oily hands
- WD40 (because you always need that shit for something)
- Vice grips
- Drill with set of drill bits and various heads
- Various screws
- Electrical tape
- Crazy glue

On the road we've had to tackle many fixes and repair jobs on the engine, body of the van and interior build. I've already told you about a number of engine fixes, but we've also had to repair cabinets, change out electrical fuses, and even built new additions to our layout we realized we wanted after living in the van for a while.

These tools also come in handy for all our sporting gear. You can tune a bike or snowboard yourself with just a few tools. Every van lifer needs a tool box and that includes you.

Van Life Chores

A tiny space gets dirty fast. It blows my mind how quickly a layer of dust accumulates on everything. How in just a day, the floor is covered in bits and gunk. How after one meal, the whole kitchen is a disaster. It's crazy how one item out of place makes the whole tiny space look like an absolute pigsty – or is that just me?!

Beyond cleaning there are a whole host of van specific chores you'll need to take care of on a regular basis. Making sure you have enough fuel, dumping black and grey water, filing fresh water tanks, emptying the garbage and recycling bins, doing laundry, you know, all those really fun adult life chores you can't escape no matter what lifestyle you choose.

Running a van is just like running a home. Somedays you don't care if the garbage is full and the laundry pile is overflowing. Other days you want your home to look spic and span. Some people really care about having everything in its place, others are happy to let chaos rule. Whatever your personal style, eventually, unless you're a hoarder in which case you need help beyond what I can offer in these pages, you're going to need to put on your big boy pants and get some shit done.

Most vanlifers I've met are surprisingly tidy. They love their home and are proud to keep it in tip top shape. They are happy to give you a tour, chat engine or build with you and get into all the dirt details of their plumbing and electrical systems. Vanlifers are some of the best, smartest people when it comes to their rigs because they've taken the time to get to know their homes, inside and out.

We can generally go a week or two before we have to commit a full day to van chores. That usually includes finding somewhere responsible to dump our garbage, grey tanks and recycling. Doing laundry, mopping the floors, and finding a nice hot shower. Daily chores include doing dishes, putting clothes away, making the bed and sweeping. Monthly chores are more like engine checks and van washes (to be honest we probably only washed our van 3 times in a whole year). After a few months you'll get into a rhythm of life and you'll have no trouble at all getting all these little tasks done.

Hot tip, buy some tablets for your grey water tank to keep grease and debris from building up. It gets vile in there without some extra help especially if you have a big tank that doesn't get dumped often. If you are going to be stationary for a while or leave your van for any length of time, be sure to empty your grey tanks first. If you don't, you'll come back to a very stinky van (that goes for garbage too but garbage is more obvious). Also, those amazing fans you installed in the roof, get very dusty. You need a special tiny Allen key to get the actual fan off to clean it. If you're concerned about air quality in your van, you're going to want to check on these often.

Generally, none of these van chores are all that hard to accomplish and a few hours of adulting leads to many hours of fun on the road.

"Whatever course you have chosen for yourself, it will not be a chore but an adventure if you bring to it a sense of the glory of striving." — David Sarnoff

Where to Travel

The world is your oyster, kind of. The first limitation of van life travel is that your rig can't fly or swim. That means unless you're ready to ship your tiny home on wheels or rent/buy a van elsewhere, you're confined to the water boarders of wherever you've decided to build your rig. This might seem limiting but there's something special about getting to explore your own backyard.

Sure, you may have lived in the same place your whole life, but there's no way you've explored every nook in every season. Heck even if you've already been to every state in America, it's highly unlikely that you've hit every national park, major city, giant ball of yarn or the home of the oldest roller coaster in the world. Have you seen the northern lights from an Inuit village or bioluminescent waters on a pristine beach? Open your mind and you'll see there are endless ways to explore your very, very, big backyard.

If you're not sure where you want to go exactly, think first about what you want to do. Do you want to play in the snow or swim in the ocean? Do you want to visit every state or focus on National Parks? Is your journey about tasting local cuisine or hiking mountains? Once you've established your dream list of adventures, you can start to pin down where you need to drive to achieve your goals. You can do this research online or in guide books but the best sources for information are always the locals.

Get near where you want to be, then ask around. Which trails are the best, which waterfalls are worth the hike, where is the water clearest, where are the best sunsets, who's got the best tacos? You'll be surprised how much you can learn and the amazing places you can explore once you get to where you're going. Places that weren't necessarily in the guidebook and are therefore generally much less crowded and touristy.

When we first started planning our adventure, Frankie's main focus for the first half of the year was snowboarding. In order to be budget friendly, we found passes that would allow us to visit as many mountains as possible for as little money as possible. We ended up purchasing two passes (Epic and Ikon) that provided us with over 70 mountains to choose from. I highly suggest buying season passes for activities you know you want to do. Whether that's a national park pass or KOA membership (we do not have one of those as it didn't make sense since we prefer to stealth camp). Do the math and see if it makes sense to shell out a few extra bucks now to save big later. This is also true for city specific passes. Most major cities have passes that let you visit multiple museums or other attractions for one fixed price. Sometimes these are a great deal, other times you'd have to cram in every attraction they offer into the time frame to make it cost effective.

For the second half of our first year on the road, I wanted to infused our lives with as much hot weather and beaches as possible after all that snowboarding.

The plan was to drive the coast from Vancouver, Canada all the way to Panama City, Panama stopping in every surf town and taco joint along the way. To plan for a multi-country trip like this you'll have to make sure you have a valid passport that is accepted in the countries you wish to travel, check on tourist visa requirements, find out what's needed for pets to cross the border (if applicable), sign up for country specific car insurance if required, research the best towns for vanlifers and make copies of all your important paperwork.

It's advised to have multiple photocopies of your driver's license and passport stashed away safely in a hidden compartment of your van. Some border checks in Central America require a copy and conveniently have a high-priced copy machine right there for you to use. Plus, if you ever lost your original documents you have backup. I would also suggest leaving copies of these documents with a trusted confidant in your home country just in case.

Of course, our plans to explore all of Central America were dashed when COVID hit but in all honestly, I am glad they were put on hold. We were planning on doing that entire trip in less than 6 months. That's driving all the way to Panama starting in May and back to Florida by Thanksgiving. We were so go go go that it didn't even dawn on us that this 9,320 mile (15,000 kilometer) adventure shouldn't be rushed.

We would have been traveling at light speed to accomplish our goal which would have made the trip less than enjoyable. Post pandemic we have really slowed down and allowed the flow of life to take over. Moving in this slow-paced way is so much more enjoyable and relaxing so I wouldn't recommend you set yourself up for any record-breaking adventures, unless that's your bag!

City versus country is a big decision for vanlifers. From my experience most of us prefer to be off-grid enjoying mother nature to the fullest – even more so since the pandemic. But there are times when city life calls and you have to answer. Stealth camping in most cities is doable even though it's complicated by signed parking restrictions. You might have to circle a few blocks or explore different neighborhoods to find legal overnight parking.

You'll also have to consider that it is much trickier to navigate tight, tiny, congested city streets in a great big rig. If you're rolling in a full-sized bus, it's likely best to stay on the outskirts of town. Cities can also bring more risk of break-ins as there aren't generally bandits roaming national parks breaking into cars. Both city life and country life can offer amazing experiences for vanlifers and a combination of both, in my option, is best.

Shipping your van is something lots of vanlifers do. Whether that's getting yourself from Central America to South America or across an ocean, there are a few factors you need to consider. First will you be able to stay on the boat with your vehicle or do you need to book a flight? For shorter ferry rides like from Baja Mexico to mainland Mexico, you remain on the boat. For longer journey's like say from Sydney, Australia to Seattle, USA, you're going to have to fly. You might also be without a vehicle/home for a number of days because the boat journey plus customs can take a month or more depending on the route.

No matter where you travel, know that you'll be in good company. There are vanlifers all over the world ready to mix and mingle with you. Some peoples van life dreams are to tour the world in 10 years. Others are happy to stay in their own backyard. We just met a couple who have been traveling for 7 years and have never left the United States. While that's not as exciting sounding for me as I'm pumped to cross borders and experience new cultures, they were full stoke on their travels.

Now that we're on the oh so fun pandemic portion of this chapter, know that each country has its own restrictions and limitations. You're going to have to fully research where you want to go and make sure that you can get things like health insurance to cover you there. Some countries, once you're in and have followed their quarantine plan, allow you to travel freely.

Others have restrictions about traveling from one area to the next. For now, it seems your backyard is the best option for van life but that can all change in a moment. Don't let this virus stifle your sense of adventure. Yes, our plans were completely derailed but we had an amazing year regardless. We met so many fascinating people and explored beautiful places we wouldn't have seen if we'd been able to stick with our original plans.

No matter where you choose to wander, know that there are well worn traveler routes all over the world. You are not the first person to decide to do van life in Australia, Spain, Thailand or any other destination. Look to those who've done it before you for guidance on where to go and then follow your heart. This chapter began with "the world is your oyster" and it really is.

Security and Safety in Your Rig and on the Road

No matter where you live or where you travel, you should always think, safety first. Van life comes with its own particular set of challenges when it comes to safety and security. You need to make sure that all your locks work and actually lock your doors whenever you leave the van. We even lock our doors when we're just chilling or sleeping in the van. If you are just settling into bed with a nice cup of tea, lock your doors, even in the middle of the forest, in all likelihood nothing will happen but better safe than sorry.

You can also get special padlocks for the outside of your van. After locking up, you use a key to lock this secondary lock that makes it practically impossible for someone to break in. These padlocks are great for the sliding door (which is apparently very easy to break into) as well as the back doors.

It is important to make sure your belongings are safely put away whenever you leave your van. If you leave your laptop or expensive camera on your front seat, you're announcing to potential thieves that you've got fancy things to steal. Whenever we leave the van, we pack away all our important belongings, put up all the window covers and close the front curtains. I'd much rather someone see a blacked-out van than be able to look in, see a pretty build and wonder what treasures are inside. Generally, people are honest, but it might be too tempting to turn down a $1,000 laptop just sitting in the front seat. Quick smash of a window and they're in the money.

When looking for places to park overnight, trust your instincts. You can find lots of known places on apps like iOverlander with reviews and insights on the location (be sure to add your own review after you stay to keep the information current). When you're out in the wilderness, you're likely safer from petty theft than downtown in an urban city. Either way, you should follow these safety precautions because you never know.

If you get to a spot for the night and it *feels* wrong, find somewhere else. If you look around the neighborhood and it doesn't *feel* safe, find somewhere else. If an extra 30 minutes of driving will put your mind at ease, it's worth it. That's also why it's good to find your overnight camping spot reasonably early. If you pull up at 1am exhausted from driving all night, you're going to park wherever, even if it doesn't feel great, just because you're tired.

When you do find the spot you want to park, always position yourself for a speedy exit - that means you should back in. If you wake up in the middle of the night to someone banging on your windows, you can easily grab your keys (which should always sleep next to you for easy access), head to the driver's seat, start the engine, and get out of there. If you have to fiddle with backing out or three-point turns (or finding your keys), you're wasting precious minutes of escape time. Plus, attacker or not, it's always safer to drive straight out of a parking spot rather than blindly backing up (hello trees!). You're much less likely to hit something when you're driving forward.

Inside your van have a fire extinguisher within easy reach as well as a smoke alarm and carbon monoxide detector. If you have a propane set up you should have a propane alarm too. Every home, including yours, needs these things.

You've got to learn how to change a flat tire and have the tools (and tire) to do it. You never know when you might pop a tire or have a rim die. Also, you really never know when something might happen in your engine or on your rig which is why as mentioned before it's so important to have a tool kit.

And finally, it goes without saying, you need insurance on your van. We have vehicle insurance and also have a renters' insurance policy at our permanent residence. Between these two plans we're covered for any car related issues like accidents and also any theft related issues like break-ins.

We spoke with a police officer recently about safety in your rig and a lot of questions came up about guns, mace, bear spray and other weapons for self-defense. As it turns out, a lot of people are worried about being attacked or just want to have something on hand to make them feel safer on the road.

Traveling with guns comes with a whole host a legalities you're going to need to research for each state and country you are traveling to. Sprays are still illegal in some places so you'll need to know the local rules, plus you're very likely to spray yourself as well when using them.

Things like knives are fine to have but you would have to get really close to your attacker to use them. Frankie and I don't have any of these precautions, except for some cooking knives and bear spray for actual bears. If it comes down to fight or flight, I'm driving out of there.

When we first got into van life our friends and family were very worried for us. They would send us articles about how unsafe Central America is, stories of people traveling by van in Mexico who were killed. There were a few people in Canada who were killed on an isolated highway as well.

Unfortunately, bad shit happens. But you don't need to live in a van for that bad shit to happen to you. Have you ever heard of home invasions? Just because houses get robbed doesn't mean people stop living in houses.

When I would turn the local news on in Brooklyn, New York there would be stories every night about people getting robbed and shot just blocks away from where I lived. It didn't faze me at all. And just because a random traveler has something negative happen to them, doesn't mean it will happen to you either.

We all hope that nothing will ever go wrong, and in all likelihood, nothing will. But, it's always best to over prepare than to wish you'd been a little more proactive.

"Life is not always perfect. Like a road, it has many bends, ups and down, but that's its beauty." — Amit Ray

The Ugly Truth of Van Life

Instagram paints a pristine picture of van life and at times, it can be just that. A beautiful sunset next to a gorgeous beach front. A hot cup of coffee as you enjoy the mist coming off plush green trees in the forest. But sometimes, you're just dealing with a heaping pile of shit (hopefully not literally).

Your home is a vehicle. A vehicle that you are likely pushing to its max. You're covering many miles on sometimes questionable roads. Your entire home is being jostled daily. Not to mention it's always exposed to the elements. There's no reprieve from boiling hot summers or freezing cold winters, torrential downpours or howling winds. One minute you can feel safe and cozy in your home, and the next like there's no way the metal box you live in could protect you from gale-force winds.

There will often be times when you have to take a break from all that relaxed living to dig around your engine to see what's going wrong. To tighten up your water lines because the connections have jiggled loose.

An hour at a hardware or auto parts store could save you five days at the mechanics down the road. It's not just a fanciful joy ride without any cares or worries. All the Instagram-able fun is punctuated by hard work, stress, motor oil and blown fuses.

You also have to find a new safe place to park your home every night. Sometimes this is easy. Sometimes this is a stressful mess. Sometimes you think you have it pulled up in your GPS and you arrive to nothing. Sometimes what sounds like a great spot turns out to be sketchy and you don't feel safe. Sometimes you'll be parked in a Walmart parking lot or other unglamorous location. I always feel best when we're staying put for a few days because I get comfortable with where we're sleeping and I don't have to think about finding somewhere new.

Another downfall of this lifestyle is that because it's desirable and many people don't have the skills to build their own rigs, you can end up paying way more than you should have to for parts and labor.

There are lots of reputable van build companies and yes you will be paying a premium for having someone else do the work. But I've seen too many van tours on YouTube where people share the prices of their crazy build ($500 for a dimmer switch, really?). When we were searching for our new van the mark ups were crazy, we had to turn down a few vans because they were so overpriced. Do your research and don't be gouged even if you're having someone else build your van.

Oh, and finally a special COVID update, people are becoming less welcoming to foreign license plates. Twice since the pandemic started, we were yelled at for "bringing the disease" to their small towns. Of course, we are socially isolated most of the time and wear masks in public but some people will see your license plate and flip out. Frankie is really the best at handling these situation as he always stays calm and cool and tries to explain (from a distance) our story and how we ended up in their town.

He reassures them that we are being safe. But sadly, you don't always get to explain yourself so just be kind and realize these people are just scared, do what you can to put them at ease and then move along.

And finally, Instagram neglects the fact that there are sometimes long stretches between showers. There are no stink lines on photoshopped photos and so you would never know that the beautiful bikini babe posting next to her van hasn't showered in a week.

For me, the positives far outweigh the negatives of van life but just like with safety, we need to be aware of the bad things in order to avoid them. Sure, it would be nice to drive around the country without a care in the world. I really hope that works out for you! I would hate for you to enter into van life thinking it was going to be all sunshine and rainbows and be incredibly disappointed at how mundane it all is at times. If you're entering van life thinking that it's going to be one great big Instagram photoshoot, you've got another thing coming.

But don't worry, you will absolutely get that beautiful photo (if you want it) and explore some of the most amazing places you've ever seen. It just won't be ever single second of ever single day unless you've got a very creative eye.

Resource Conservation

After a short timing living in a van, you'll come to deeply appreciate how limited your resources are. You only have so many gallons of water. Your propane will run out. You're constantly filling the gas/diesel tank. Cloudy days will take all the juice from your solar electrical system.

It's amazing how disconnected we become to these realities when they don't impact our daily lives. When I was living in a house, sure I thought about conserving water, low flow toilets and shutting off the faucet while I brushed my teeth. But that didn't stop me from showering every day or running the dishwasher every night. Now that I only have so many gallons, I barely use any water to even wash my dishes. When I wash my face, I turn the water on and off and on and off to use as little as possible.

We're always looking at our battery levels to decide, can we turn on the blender? Should we park in the shade where it will be cooler or in the sun where our batteries can charge fully? We had a pretty robust solar system and still ran low. When we had AGM batteries we had to monitor and make sure not to use more than 50% of the stored power.

For our next van build, we are switching to lithium batteries that we can run down to zero without worry. But even lithium batteries won't charge when the clouds come in.

It would be great if we could run our actual engine on renewable resources but for now, the majority of vans require gas or diesel. We did find a fully electric Promaster but it could only go 100 miles before needing to recharge and we like to go way off grid. Many rigs get terrible gas mileage which means it will cost a lot to travel long distances. That's why lots of vanlifers rely on secondary vehicles to get around town. To conserve fuel in their gas guzzling rig, they park their home in a spot for weeks at a time and then use their tow behind vehicle or motorcycle to run errands and get around.

Your cashflow might be a limited resource as well. We love to stretch every dollar to essentially extend our traveling life as long as possible. We cook our own meals, shop at discount stores, avoid unnecessary expenditures and always choose the frugal option. We would rather 10 amazing dinners at delicious taco stands than 1 gourmet dinner at a fancy restaurant and 1000 nights of boondocking over 50 nights at camp grounds. That's our style though and yours may be different.

Van life has gotten us closer to nature than we ever imagined. We are constantly in awe of the beautiful places we get to visit and the amazing vistas we get to park next to. As we walk along the trails and beaches and enjoy the campsites, it's hard not to notice the impact us as humans are having on the planet. Random trash strewn on picturesque trails. Waterways with unnaturally dense foam from the chemicals in it. Dunes eroding, forests devastated by fire, ski resorts with no snow in the winter.

Being this close to the earth not only shows her beauty but also her pain. Anything we can do, any resource we can conserve to make our footprint smaller, we will gladly do just to enjoy her splendor for one more day. This is also why 10% of the earnings from this book as well as our YouTube channel are donated to environmental causes.

"Some changes look negative on the surface but you will soon realize that space is being created in your life for something to new emerge." — Eckhart Tolle

People in the Wild

Van life attracts all kinds of people. Frankie and I are the social type. We see a van life van, and want to know who lives it in. What's their story? How does their build look? Where have they traveled? How did they come to this lifestyle? It's so interesting for us to meet people who share our passions and way of life. But of course, being extremely friendly and personable attracts all kinds of crazy. Here are just a few of our encounters with people in the wild.

From a guy living in the hardware store parking lot who asked us "did acid find you or did you find acid?" the answer to that is neither; to the retired army veteran traveling with his young family in a fabulous RV. We've met people escaping wildfires in California and travelers who've been on the road and loving it for years. Vanlifers come in all shapes, sizes, ages, and colors, say hello to your fellow nomads!

The first couple we met on the road were working at a ski resort. This seasonal work paid for them to travel the rest of the year. At this point we were both so excited to meet each other because neither of us had ever met another vanlifer. We were in Ontario, Canada where van life isn't as big as in say California, USA. It was a thrill to take our first tour ever of someone else's van. We had only seen rigs online, never in person. We chatted with them for hours and then parked next to each other for the night. In the morning the conversation enthusiastically resumed and we had a great time skiing with them that day.

Once we got to the West Coast of the United States, our encounters with vanlifers increased tenfold. It seemed every town we visited was a known van life town. Every boondocking location was well traveled. We met solo travelers, couples, retirees and families all loving life on the road.

When we got to Oregon and decided to stay in the area for a while, we met a whole group of travelers, with rigs of all shapes and sizes and spent many nights exploring all corners of the state together. This group even put together a meetup calling all nomads to gather. We ended up with over 100 rigs from all over the country coming to the same campsite for an extra-long weekend of campfires and connection.

In Olympic National Park in Washington, we randomly said hello to a fellow nomad in a grocery store parking lot. We ended up caravanning with him for 6 days and built such a strong bond with him we now consider him family. If you're familiar with our vlogs you'll know Uncle Kevin from his many appearances. This friendship started with an awkward hello and will continue with many more adventures on the road.

While wandering the Redwood trails in California, we connected with another couple who just so happened to recognize us from YouTube. That 3-hour conversation led to 2 nights in the most perfect campground having deep conversations about life. Since then, we keep in touch and meet up wherever we can. These folks inspire us to be better and those kinds of people can truly change your life.

No matter where you meet, you already have something in common, you are vanlifers. We make a point to say hello to every nomad we see and have yet to meet anyone rude. Ever notice how you're the best version of yourself when you're on vacation? Well, that's how vanlifers live every day of their lives. Of course they are going to want to say hi and make a connection. Don't be shy, say hello! You might just be meeting your new best friend.

"Life is beautiful not because of the things we see or do. Life is beautiful because of the people we meet." — Simon Sinek

Emergency Escape Vehicle

One of the things we joked about when building our van was that it would be the perfect vehicle to run away from the zombie apocalypse. In just a few hours of driving, you can be totally isolated in the wilderness with everything needed to survive for weeks. Then, COVID-19 swept the globe. Although we're incredibly grateful that this virus doesn't cause humans to rise from the dead and eat each other, it certainly stunted many vanlifers travel plans (along with causing countless less trivial tragedies).

When the crisis first hit, we happened to be visiting a friend in Tahoe, California. He was kind enough to take us along to Costco, Trader Joe's, Safeway and Home Depot to load up on $300 worth of canned goods, fresh food and bleach cleaners. I was worried all that food wouldn't fit in the van but I stocked our cupboards with ease filling them with canned beans, tomatoes, nuts, seeds, dried fruit, pasta, rice, oats and more, then stuffing our fridge with vegan meat, fresh fruits and vegetables.

We also filled up our 36-gallon water tank, a volume we can make last for weeks, longer if we're being extra careful. Because we also have a water filtration system, we can refill with creek water if need be and filter out any impurities. There is also a tool you can get that unlocks locked water sources on buildings. If something were to really hit the fan that could be very handy but I don't feel right using it when everything is kosher and there are free legal sources everywhere.

If you're really planning on going off grid you have to think about additional non-perishable food storage. Do you have a stash of canned goods somewhere not in your regular rotation that could be left unused in case going off grid is completely necessary? Not to be a fear monger, but when COVID first hit we saw the issues with supply chain and grocery store madness (toilet paper? Really?!). If you're planning to escape "the end of the world" you're going to need a few things.

Perhaps an axe and saw for firewood. A way to start a fire that won't run out like a flint. Candles and sleeping gear for warmth if you lose electricity. Extra fuel, water and food. Tools to repair your rig. You might also want to have some hunting and foraging skills, being able to trap your dinner or to pick wild berries that won't kill you are great skills to have. You should always have a book or two on hand that can explain survival skills to you in case of emergency and no cell signal.

When COVID happened, we were able to leave the big city and head out to rural areas. We could have waited out the storm in a beautiful wooded area. Instead, we opted to travel to Frankie's sister's house outside of Seattle so that we would be close to family (and working plumbing). Sure, if we had our own home, we would have just bunkered down there, but community is one of the most powerful ways to boost our health and longevity. Plus, when you have community working together, cooking, cleaning and taking care of each other, everyone is better off.

In hindsight, especially after entering week three of an indefinite shelter in place order, we wished we had taken more time getting there. In the moment it seemed like the best thing to do, get to safety as quickly as possible. But our wanderlust started burning and it became increasingly hard not to dream about the freedom of the open road. But then I read what others were going through, facilities closed, showers and toilets sparse, grocery stores in small towns empty, and I was glad we made the decision we did.

Through our online vanlifer community, it's clear that the ability for us to weather the pandemic varies greatly depending on each individual's situation and van build. Many vanlifers rely on gyms or other public places for showers; these were all closed. With camp grounds closed, some couldn't find safe places to park their larger rigs. Others didn't have the luxury of friends or family to stay with.

Imagine if you were on the other side of the world and had to leave your beloved van behind to get back to the safety of your own country. With health insurance companies dropping coverage for people outside their home countries some had little choice. We were still on our own continent so could drive to safety.

If you decide to ship your van, be sure to get it shipment ready by removing all your valuables, emptying your fridge and triple securing everything. I've heard stories of vanlifers whose rigs were raided while in transit or at the customs yard but thankfully they didn't have anything worth stealing inside.

Another consideration about shipping your rig is that you might end up delayed because of it. If your rig gets held up in customs you could be spending an additional week or more back and forth on paperwork trying to free your vehicle. We're seeing online now, 8 months later, people are just not getting their homes back. Be sure you have a plan for somewhere to stay while waiting for your rig and relax and enjoy the ride, you'll get her back eventually.

It's a trying time for everyone but what's clear is that without some survival skills or the ability to live off grid, your escape vehicle won't provide much safety after all. And after living with a poorly built toilet for over a year, our next build will definitely have something more legit.

"Not I - Not anyone else, can travel that road for you, You must travel it for yourself." — Walt Whitman

The Beautiful Side of Van Life

The van life community is truly one of a kind. It accepts people from all walks of life, all races and religions. Though our travels, Frankie and I have had the pleasure of meeting many wonderful people. We've developed bonds that will last a lifetime. We've shared meals with strangers we now call friends. Vanlifers are generally kind and generous, they are curious to see what your build looks like and interested to hear your tales from the road.

Whenever we see a rig, we wave and say hello. Often, we find ourselves in 30+ minute conversations in the grocery store parking lot talking van and making plans to meet down the road. If you're outgoing and friendly, you'll have no issues making friends along the way.

Sometimes the best way to connect with other people, aside from approaching them at a Safeway, is to go to known camping locations you find on iOverlander or other apps.

You can also tryout campgrounds although you might find more retirees and weekend warriors there than true vanlifers. Just like if you were backpacking across Europe and staying in hostels, staying on Bureau of Land Management and national forest lands known for boondocking, you're more likely to meet likeminded travelers.

The online van life community is booming. There are endless hashtags and Facebook groups where you can find out about meetups and connect with other vanlifers. We've met up with plenty of people we connected with online and have never had a bad experience sitting around a campfire swapping stories. You just have to put yourself out there and you'll be amazed at the response.

Of course, the most beautiful side of van life is the places you get to explore. The world is a vast and magical ecosystem. Hidden forest alcoves and sparse mountain tops call to us. The energy you get from visiting these places is peaceful and energetic at the same time. You'll find places you want to stay forever and some you never want to share with anyone else because they are too perfect.

Because you have endless time to explore, you can actually slow down and find the true beauty in a place. Say you show up to an area you were excited about but it's scheduled to rain for a few days, no worries. Find a place to camp and get cozy in your tiny home until the rain lifts. Unlike that 2 weeks of vacation per year your job used to give you, you can take all the time you want exploring an area or not. If you get somewhere and decide you don't enjoy it, move on.

Most of us have forgotten what day of the week it is and are simply in the flow of life. Eat when you're hungry, explore when you're adventurous, sleep under the stars. If you've set yourself up as I've described in this book, you'll have no problems enjoying this world rain or shine, wherever your tiny home takes you. And isn't that the most beautiful part of van life?

"We were meant to explore this earth like children do, unhindered by fear, propelled by curiosity and a sense of discovery. Allow yourself to see the world through new eyes and know there are amazing adventures here for you." — Laurel Bleadon Maffei

Happy Trails

I hope this book has helped you feel more confident about your van life adventure. Some people take years to plan out their adventure, others buy a van and are on the road the next day.

Each person's journey is unique but there's one thing we all have in common - adventure is calling.

If you have any questions, want to meet up along the way, or want to share your van life adventures with us, feel free to reach out via social media @fnavanlife or through our website www.fnavanlife.com.

Happy trails my nomad friend,

XO Alex, Frankie & Paco too!

Resources

Here's a handy summary of things to help you continue your van life adventures:

Our Socials:

- YouTube www.youtube.com/fnavanlife
- Facebook www.facebook.com/fnavanlife
- Instagram www.instagram.com/fnavanlife
- Podcast www.anchor.fm/fnavanlife

Download our Budget Guide Here:

https://fnavanlife.com/budget-to-quit-your-job-for-extended-travel/

My Other Book
- Secrets of a Successful Executive Assistant - https://amzn.to/2yOGtO1

Index

Introduction 3

Why Van Life? 9

Quit Your Job to Live the Dream 15

The Budget 21

Your Rig 29

Gathering Funds for Your Van 39

Earn Free Money 43

The Build 49

Big Mistakes to Avoid in Your Build 63

Electrical 69

Insulation and Heat 75

Plumbing 81

Layout 89

Leaving Your Life Behind 95

Minimalist Lifestyle 99

Daily Costs on The Road 103

Travel Companions 111

Where to Go to The Bathroom 119

Where to Sleep 131

Where to Shower 141

Where to Get Your Mail 149

Laundry 153

Leave No Trace Principals 157

Breakdowns 163

Earn Money to Extend Travel 171

Become a Digital Nomad 179

Finding Internet 187

Night Driving 193

Regular Maintenance 199

Tools You Need 203

Van Life Chores 205

Where to Travel 209

Security and Safety in Your Rig and on the Road 217

The Ugly Truth of Van Life 223

Resource Conservation 227

People in the Wild 231

Emergency Escape Vehicle 235

The Beautiful Side of Van Life 241

Happy Trails 245

Resources 246

Index 247

Printed in Great Britain
by Amazon